· LATTER DAY KIDS ·

Doctrine & Covenants

STUDY COMPANION FOR FAMILIES

WEEKLY LESSONS + VIDEOS + ACTIVITIES

2025

DEDICATION:

This book is dedicated to you! To the parents, teachers, and leaders who are dilignetly leading the rising generation to Christ.

ISBN: 9798342895712

Lessons and activites created by Jared Austin
Layout design by Marcie Austin

www.latterdaykids.com

· LATTER DAY KIDS ·

Doctrine & Covenants

STUDY COMPANION FOR FAMILIES

WEEKLY LESSONS + VIDEOS + ACTIVITIES

2025

TIPS AND FAQ'S:

IS THERE A WAY TO VIEW THE VIDEOS WITHOUT HAVING TO GO TO YOUTUBE?

Yes! Purchasing this manual gives you instant and unrestricted access to download all of the videos directly to your device (ad free)! Each lesson contains a QR code to download the relevant video. Simply scan the QR code and download the video! Use the QR code at the beginning of this book to download all of the videos at once.

HOW SHOULD I USE THE LESSONS?

The lessons are designed to make it easy for anyone to teach gospel topics to young children. (If you have older children in your household, we recommend inviting those children to try leading the lessons!) Simply follow the script to experience and learn about the concepts together with your children. It is our hope that the lesson activities will open the door to meaningful reflection and Spirit-guided conversations with your children. This is where the important learning will take place.

WHO MAKES THESE LESSONS?

The lessons were all created by Jared Austin. Jared is a former public school teacher with a Master's Degree in Curriculum and Instruction and 13 years of teaching experience. Jared specializes in making big concepts relatable and memorable for small children. These lessons are designed to be a supplement to the "Come Follow Me - Home and Church" manual produced by the Church of Jesus Chirst of Latter Day Saints. Before using the materials in this book, it is recommended to use the scriptures as the primary resource, and then to use the Come Follow Me manual produced by the Church as a secondary resource.

WHAT MATERIALS WILL I NEED TO TEACH THESE LESSONS?

Other than personal prayer and study, the lessons require very little preparation. All object lessons use common household items to make preparation easy and inexpensive.

WHY DO YOU COVER ONLY ONE TOPIC IN THE MANUAL EACH WEEK?

Children learn, remember, and apply concepts with much greater success when they can focus on one topic at a time. During a single lesson, children will learn about one topic through a variety of learning activities (object lessons, kinesthetic activities, parables, storytelling, discussion questions, repetition, and art activities). We would love to provide a complete lesson bundle each week for each topic, but for now, our limited resources require that we focus on just one topic per week.

HOW DO YOU DECIDE WHICH TOPIC YOU WILL COVER EACH WEEK?

We try to use our best judgment with several factors in mind. Some of the things we consider are: Clarity and thoroughness of the scripture passages related to the topic, whether that topic was covered already in a previous week, appropriateness and relevance of the topic for young children, etc. We highly encourage parents and leaders to seek the guidance of the Spirit when selecting topics to cover (rather than simply using the topic that was selected by Latter Day Kids).

CONTENTS:

CONTENTS:

CONTENTS:

CONTENTS:

LATTER DAY KIDS VIDEO DOWNLOADS

Scan this QR code to download all Latter Day Kids videos for 2025!

KARAOKE VIDEO DOWNLOADS

Scan this QR code to download all karaoke videos for 2025!

INDIVIDUAL VIDEO DOWNLOADS

Separate QR codes for are also provided in each lesson to download the individual videos one at a time.

This page intentionally left blank.

Week 1: Dec 30 - Jan 5

 ## THE RESTORATION

 TOPIC | The Gospel of Jesus Christ is Restored

OPENING SONG "We Thank Thee O God for a Prophet"

INTRODUCTION:

Ask children the following question:

What time is it right now? (*Allow children to search for a watch, clock, or mobile device to find the answer.*)

After children have completed the activity, discuss the following:

1) When you wanted to know what time it was, did you just sit still and do nothing? Or did you look around for something? (*Discuss*)

2) What did you look for? Where did you go? (*Looked for a clock*)

3) Why did you look for a clock? (*Because we know the clock can tell us the time!*)

4) Can a clock teach us about Heavenly Father or Jesus Christ? (*No*)

5) If we want to learn about Heavenly Father and Jesus Christ, what should we look around for? Who should we go to? (*Study the scriptures, study the teachings of the prophets, watch general conferences, pray to Heavenly Father, etc.*)

Explain: Just like we go to the clock to see what time it is, we can go to Heavenly Father in prayer when we have an important question! In the scriptures, Heavenly Father has told us lots of times to "ask," and we will receive.

VIDEO:

Say: "We are going to watch a video about Joseph Smith when he was looking for an answer to a very important question. See if you can find out what Joseph Smith wanted to know, and see if you can find out what he did to find the answer to his question."

[Watch Video: "The First Vision | Come Follow Me Lesson for Kids"]

Discuss the following questions after watching the video:

    1) What did Joseph want to know? *(what church to join)*

    2) How did Joseph Smith find the answer? *(Prayed to ask Heavenly Father)*

    3) Did Joseph Smith do anything before he decided to pray? What did he do? *(Read the scriptures, asked other people, visited different churches, etc.)*

    4) Joseph found a scripture that gave him an idea. Do you remember what the scripture said to do? *(Ask God)*

SCRIPTURE:

Read the verses below and discuss the questions that follow.

[Read James 1:5]

After reading the verses together, discuss the following questions:

    1) What does it mean when it says "if any of you lack wisdom?" *(Discuss)*

    2) How can we ask God something? What do we have to do? *(Discuss)*

    3) What does it mean when it says "it shall be given him." *(Discuss)*

    4) What do you think Heavenly Father wants us to do when we want to know about something? *(Discuss)*

    5) Can you think of other stories in the scriptures when someone needed to ask God for something? *(Discuss)*

[Read James 1:6]

1) What do you think "ask in faith" means? (Discuss)

2) What do you think "nothing wavering" means? What is "wavering?" (*Invite children to walk across the room and show you what they think "wavering" looks like*)

3) What do you think it means to not waver when we are asking something? (*Invite children to walk across the room and demonstrate a direct path, not wavering*)

4) How did Joseph Smith show that he was not wavering? (*He worked for a long time to find an answer to his question, he kept asking and really wanted to know.*)

ACTIVITY:

[Pass out activity pages]

Color and cut out the images of the "standing" Joseph Smith, and the three churches. Fold on the dotted lines to create stand-up figures. Spread out the church buildings and then help Joseph "walk" from one church to the next in search of his answer. Color the scene of the first vision. Remind children that we can all ask Heavenly Father things in prayer, just like Joseph Smith did.

♡ TESTIMONY:

Bear testimony of the truths found in the scriptures.

This page intentionally left blank.

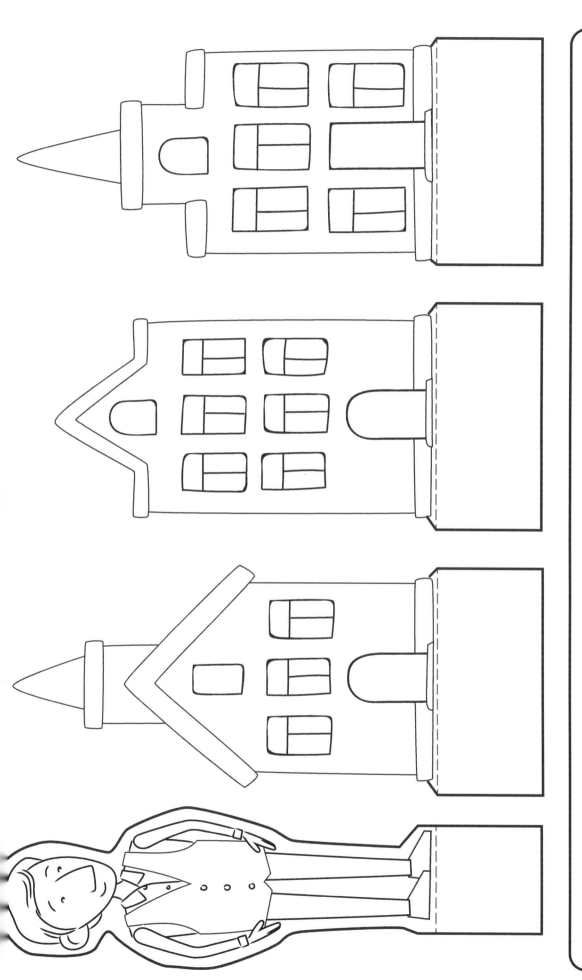

Color and cut out the images of Joseph Smith, and the three churches. Fold on the dotted lines to create stand-up figures. Spread out the church buildings and then help Joseph "walk" from one church to the next in search of his answer. Color the scene of the first vision. Remind children that we can all ask Heavenly Father things in prayer, just like Joseph Smith did.

www.latterdaykids.com

This page intentionally left blank.

"If any of you lack wisdom, let him ask of God, that giveth to all men liberally, and upbraideth not; and it shall be given him." -James 1:5

www.latterdaykids.com

This page intentionally left blank.

LATTER DAY
KIDS

Week 2: Jan 6-12

📖 D&C 1

💡 TOPIC | The Voice of Warning

🎵 OPENING SONG "The Iron Rod"

✏️ PREPARATION:

Find the "Voice of Warning Intro Activity" page. Cut on the dotted lines to make 4 warning signs. You will also need a physical set of scriptures for each child.

💬 INTRODUCTION:

Hold up each sign (from the "Voice of Warning Intro Activity") one at a time, and discuss the following questions for each sign.

1) Have you seen a warning like this before? (*Discuss.*)

2) Do you know what it means? (*Discuss.*)

3) What could happen if someone ignored this warning? (*Discuss.*)

4) What will happen if someone chooses to obey this warning? (*Discuss.*)

Hold up all of the signs together and explain: Today we are going to learn about warnings. These signs warn us about physical danger. Physical dangers can hurt our bodies. But there are also spiritual dangers. Spiritual dangers can hurt our spirits.

Now, hold up the scriptures and explain: God has given us warnings through His prophets to protect us from spiritual danger. These warnings can be found in the scriptures.

9

▶ VIDEO:

Now hand out the scriptures to each child so that they can hold them.

Say: "Now we are going to watch a video about warnings. Ted the truck driver must deliver his load to the warehouse safely. He sees some warning signs while he is driving. Let's watch, and see if he listens to the warnings!"

[Watch Video: "Warning Signs | Animated Scripture Lesson for Kids"

Discuss the following questions after watching the video:

1) What warnings did Ted see while he was driving? (*Seep Grade Hill Ahead, Winding Road, Land Ends: Merge Left, Road Construction Ahead.*)

2) Did Ted obey the warnings that he saw? (*Yes.*)

3) What could have happened if Ted ignored the warnings? (*Discuss.*)

4) Where can we find warnings about spiritual danger? (*In the scriptures.*)

5) What can happen if we ignore the warnings of spiritual danger? (*Our spirits can be hurt.*)

SCRIPTURE

Read the following scriptures and discuss the questions that follow.

[Doctrine and Covenants 1:4]

4 And the voice of warning shall be unto all people, by the mouths of my disciples, whom I have chosen in these last days.

1) Who is the voice of warning for? (*All people.*)

2) Is the warning for you too? (*Yes.*)

3) How does God give His warnings to us? (*Through his disciples.*)

4) Who wrote the scriptures in the Doctrine and Covenants? (*Joseph Smith.*)

[3 Nephi 14:24-27]

24 Therefore, whoso heareth these sayings of mine and doeth them, I will liken him unto a wise man, who built his house upon a rock—

25 And the rain descended, and the floods came, and the winds blew, and beat upon that house; and it fell not, for it was founded upon a rock.

26 And every one that heareth these sayings of mine and doeth them not shall be likened unto a foolish man, who built his house upon the sand—

27 And the rain descended, and the floods came, and the winds blew, and beat upon that house; and it fell, and great was the fall of it.

1) Who is speaking in these verses? *(Jesus.)*

2) What did He say it would be like if we do what He has taught us? *(Like a wise man who built his house on a firm foundation.)*

3) What did He warn it will be like if we don't do what He has taught us? *(Like a foolish man who built his house on a sandy foundation.)*

4) Can you think of any spiritual warnings in the scriptures? What has God told us to do? What has God told us not to do? *(Discuss teachings from the scriptures.)*

✏ ACTIVITY PAGES:

[Pass out the Coloring Page]

Invite the children to color the scene from "The Voice of Warning." Read the scripture that is on the coloring page with the children. Use this time to talk about heeding the voice of warning that God has given to us through his prophets!

♡ TESTIMONY:

Bear testimony of the truths found in the scriptures.

This page intentionally left blank.

This page intentionally left blank.

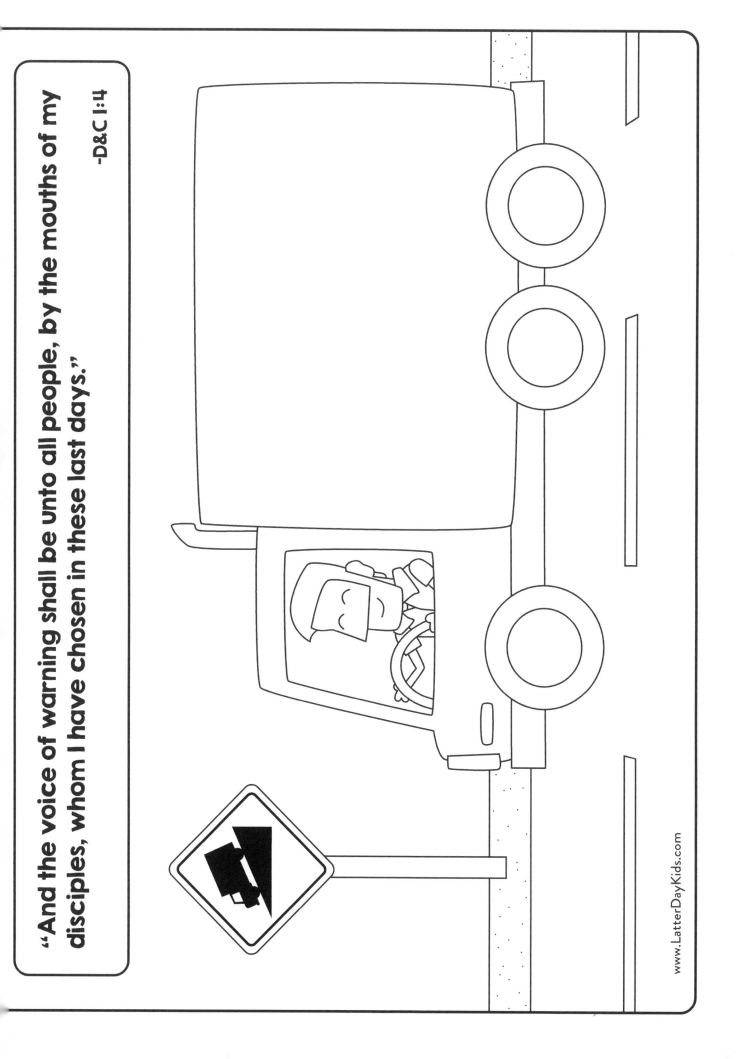

"And the voice of warning shall be unto all people, by the mouths of my disciples, whom I have chosen in these last days."

-D&C 1:4

This page intentionally left blank.

Week 3: Jan 13 - 19

📖 JOSEPH SMITH-HISTORY 1:1-26

| 💡 **TOPIC** | My Servant Joseph |

| 🎵 **OPENING SONG** | "Praise to the Man" |

📝 PREPARATION:

You will need a strong stick or pole (such as a broom handle).

💬 INTRODUCTION:

As for two volunteers to do a stick pull! Participants sit on the floor across from one another. Each person's feet should be against their opponent's feet. Each person holds onto the stick and tries to pull the other person off the ground by pulling on the stick.

Invite others to play until everyone who wants to play has had an opportunity.

Now ask the following questions:

1) Can you guess who liked to play this game? (*Joseph Smith.*)

2) Can you guess who the champion stick puller of Hancock County, Illinois was in 1843? (*Joseph Smith.*)

Explain: God called Joseph Smith to be a Prophet. God prepared and guided Joseph throughout his life. Today, we are going to learn about the life of Joseph Smith and some of the things that God did for Joseph to prepare him for his calling.

▶ VIDEO:

Say: "Now we are going to watch a video about Joseph Smith. See how many things you can remember about his life."

[Watch Video: "My Servant Joseph | Animated Scripture Lesson for Kids"]

Discuss the following questions after watching the video:

1) How many kids were in Joseph Smith's family? *(Eleven.)*

2) What lessons do you think Joseph learned from his brothers and sisters? *(Discuss.)*

3) What were some of the jobs the kids had to help with on the farm? *(Chores, building fences, harvesting maple syrup.)*

4) What lessons do you think Joseph learned from working on the farm? *(Discuss.)*

5) What happened to Joseph's leg when he was seven years old? *(It became infected, and he had to endure a painful surgery to save his leg. He had to use crutches for the next 3 years.)*

6) What do you think Joseph learned from this experience? *(Discuss.)*

7) What book did Joseph use to practice reading? *(The family copy of the bible.)*

8) What do you think Joseph learned from studying the bible? *(Discuss.)*

9) Think about what you and your family have experienced over the last year. What are some lessons you can learn from your experiences? *(Discuss.)*

SCRIPTURE:

Read the following scriptures and discuss the questions that follow.

[Read Joseph Smith History 1:10]

10 In the midst of this war of words and tumult of opinions, I often said to myself: What is to be done? Who of all these parties are right; or, are they all wrong together? If any one of them be right, which is it, and how shall I know it?

1) What was Joseph trying to do? *(He was trying to decide what church to join.)*

2) What was the "war of words and tumult of opinions" about? (*Religion and who was right.*)

3) Did Joseph know what to do? (*No.*)

[Read Joseph Smith History 1:11]

11 While I was laboring under the extreme difficulties caused by the contests of these parties of religionists, I was one day reading the Epistle of James, first chapter and fifth verse, which reads: If any of you lack wisdom, let him ask of God, that giveth to all men liberally, and upbraideth not; and it shall be given him.

1) Was it easy for him to solve this problem? Or extremely difficult? (*Extremely difficult.*)

2) Can you think of anything in your life that is causing extreme difficulty for you right now? (*Discuss.*)

3) What was Joseph Smith reading while he was facing this difficult challenge? (*The bible.*)

4) What did the scriptures teach Joseph? (*That he could ask God for help with his problem.*)

5) Do you think this scripture is for us too? Can we ask God for help when we have a difficult problem? (*Yes!*)

[Read D&C 124:125]

125 I give unto you my servant Joseph to be a presiding elder over all my church, to be a translator, a revelator, a seer, and prophet.

1) What are some of the things that God called Joseph Smith to do? (Be a presiding elder, a translator, a revelator, and a prophet.)

 ## ACTIVITY PAGES:

[Pass out the Coloring Page]

Invite the children to color the Joseph Smith Coloring Page. Use this time to talk about how God prepared Joseph Smith for his calling, and how we can learn and grow from our experiences.

♡ TESTIMONY:

Bear testimony of the truths found in the scriptures.

This page intentionally left blank.

"I give unto you my servant Joseph to be a presiding elder over all my church, to be a translator, a revelator, a seer, and prophet."

-D&C 124:125

This page intentionally left blank.

Week 4: Jan 20 - 26

📖 D&C 2; JOSEPH SMITH-HISTORY 1:27-65

🔆 TOPIC | The Sealing Power

🎵 OPENING SONG "I Love to See the Temple"

📝 PREPARATION:

You will need a bowl of ice cubes and a towel.

💬 INTRODUCTION:

Spread the towel on the floor or on a table. Place the bowl of ice in the center of the towel and invite everyone to gather around. Invite everyone to take two ice cubes out of the bowl and to squeeze them together as hard as they can for 10 seconds!

After ten seconds, many of the ice cubes should be stuck together! Now ask everyone to try to pull the ice cubes apart to see how strong the bond is.

After you complete the activity, discuss the following questions:

1) Did anyone here have enough power to bond the ice cubes together? (*Discuss.*)

2) Was it a strong bond? Or could it be broken easily? (*It was not a very strong bond, and it could be broken easily.*)

3) Do you think the bond you made with the ice cubes will last for a long time? (*No.*)

4) Do you think Heavenly Father has the power to bind things together? (*Yes.*)

5) If Heavenly Father wanted to bind something together, how strong do you think he could make that bond? (*Discuss.*)

6) If Heavenly Father wanted to bind something together, how long do you think that bond would last? (*Discuss.*)

Explain: In the scriptures, we learn that Heavenly Father has power to bind families together forever! We can go to the temple and our families can be sealed together with the priesthood power.

▶ VIDEO:

Say: "Now we are going to watch a video about welding links! Watch closely, and see if you can learn what welding is."

[Watch Video: "A Welding Link | Animated Scripture Lesson for Kids"]

Discuss the following questions after watching the video:

1) What does "welding" mean? (*It's when you melt two pieces of metal together into one piece.*)

2) When chain links are welded together the right way, are they weak or strong? (*They are very strong.*)

3) What can we do to bind our family together with strong welding links? (*We can go to the temple and be sealed together with the priesthood power!*)

4) If Heavenly Father seals our family together with his power, is it a weak bond? Or a strong bond? (*A strong bond.*)

5) How long do you think it can last? (*Forever!*)

📖 SCRIPTURE:

Read the following scripture verses and discuss the questions that follow.

[Read Matthew 16:19]

19 And I will give unto thee the keys of the kingdom of heaven: and whatsoever thou shalt bind on earth shall be bound in heaven...

1) God has given His sealing priesthood power to someone. Guess who? (*The Apostle Peter.*)

2) If something is sealed with the power of God, will it still be sealed in Heaven? (*Yes.*)

[Read D&C 132:46]

46 And verily, verily, I say unto you, that whatsoever you seal on earth shall be sealed in heaven; and whatsoever you bind on earth, in my name and by my word, saith the Lord, it shall be eternally bound in the heavens;

1) God has given His priesthood power to someone else. Do you know who? (*Joseph Smith.*)

2) If something is sealed with the power of God, will it still be sealed in Heaven? (*Yes.*)

[Read D&C 2:1-2]

1 Behold, I will reveal unto you the Priesthood, by the hand of Elijah the prophet, before the coming of the great and dreadful day of the Lord.

2 And he shall plant in the hearts of the children the promises made to the fathers, and the hearts of the children shall turn to their fathers.

1) Which prophet had the sealing priesthood power in this verse? (*Elijah the prophet.*)

2) What can we do if we want our family to be sealed together with God's priesthood power? (*We can go to the temple and be sealed together with the priesthood power!*)

✏️ ACTIVITY PAGES:

[Pass out the Activity Pages]

Help the children write the names of family members on the "links" on the activity page. Help them cut out the links and then "weld" them together into a chain with tape or a stapler. Invite the children to color the scene from the video. You can also use this time as an opportunity to discuss God's sealing power and the importance of sealing our families together with a strong "welding link."

♡ TESTIMONY:

Bear testimony of the truths found in the scriptures.

This page intentionally left blank.

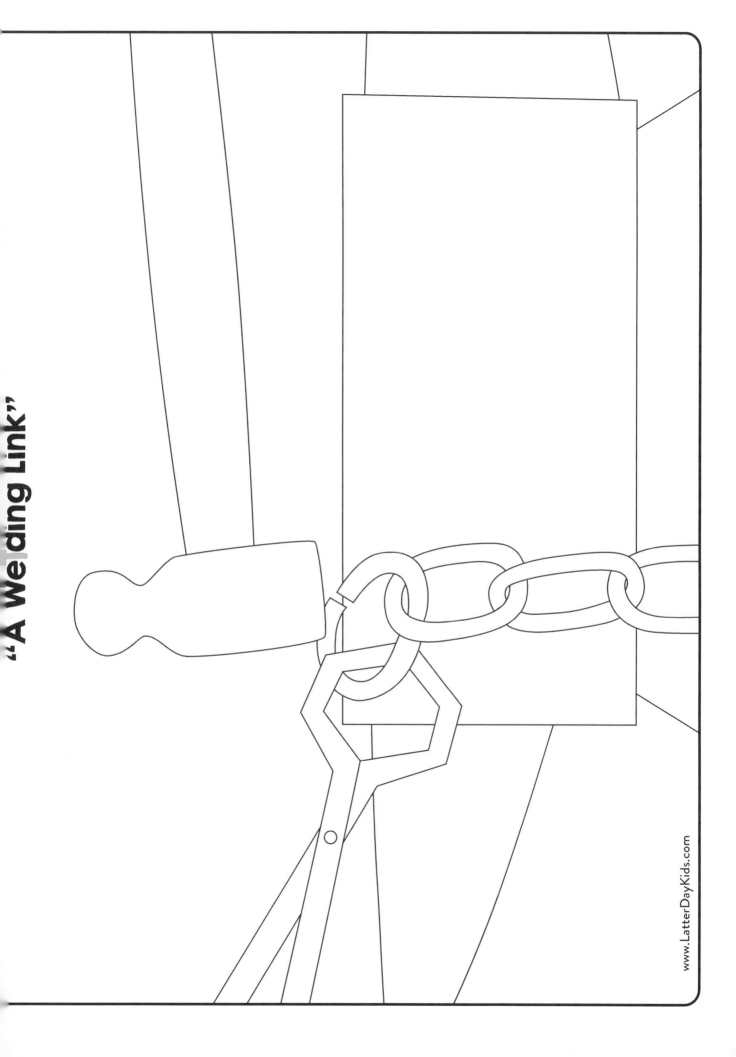

"A Welding Link"

This page intentionally left blank.

Family History "Welding Links" Activity

Write the name of a family member on each "link." Cut on the dotted lines, and then "weld" the links together with tape or a stapler to make a paper chain!

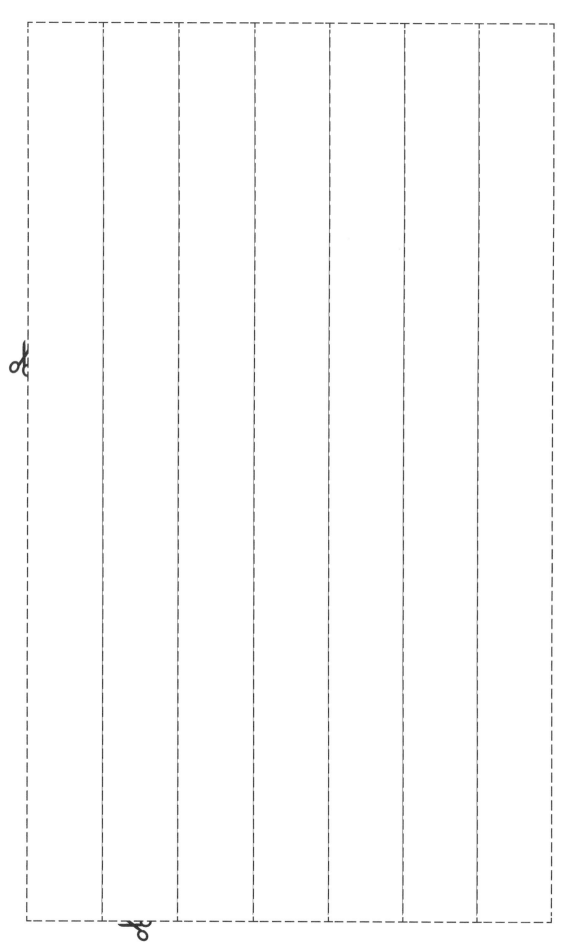

This page intentionally left blank.

Week 5: Jan 27 - Feb 2

 D&C 3-5

 TOPIC | The Field is White

 **OPENING SONG** "Called to Serve"

✐ PREPARATION:

A cup of dry whole wheat kernels, a towel, and an image of Jesus Christ. (If you don't have any whole wheat kernels, you can substitute for anything else that is small that you have a lot of - such as popcorn kernels, dry beans, etc.)

💬 INTRODUCTION:

Lay the towel on a table or on the floor, then place the image of Jesus in the center of the towel and spread the kernels all over the towel around the image. Ask for a volunteer. Invite the volunteer to use their hands and "gather" as many kernels as they can in ten seconds by placing them on the image of Jesus one at a time (one by one)!

Now repeat the timed activity, but this time everyone gets to help! When time runs out, leave everything in place

Discuss the following questions after you have completed the activity.

1) How much were you able to gather when only one person was gathering? (*Discuss.*)

2) How much were you able to gather when more people were gathering? (*Discuss!*)

3) If the kernels represent people, what do you think the gathering represents? (*Bringing people to Jesus Christ.*)

4) (Point to the seeds that are lying on the image of Jesus.) Do you think Jesus Christ loves these people? *(Yes!)*

5) (Now point to the kernels that are still on the towel.) Do you think Jesus Christ also loves these people? *(Yes!)*

6) What do you think Jesus wants us to do? *(He calls us to help bring others unto Him).*

Explain: Today, our lesson is about faith, doing God's work, and bringing others to Jesus Christ!

▶ VIDEO:

Say: "We are going to watch a video about helping others come to Jesus Christ! In the scriptures, Jesus said the field is white already to harvest. When you watch the video, see if you can find out what it means when the field is white."

[Watch Video: "The Field is White | Animated Scripture Lesson for Kids"]

Discuss the following questions after watching the video:

1) What does it mean when the field is white? *(It means the wheat field is ready to harvest.)*

2) When the field is white, who does the farmer send to gather the wheat? *(The workers.)*

3) Who does Heavenly Father send to help gather people and help bring them to Christ? *(She kept caring for the seeds.)*

4) Does Heavenly Father want anyone to be left out? *(No, He loves all of us very much and He wants every one of us to come to Jesus Christ.)*

📖 SCRIPTURE:

Read the following scripture verses and discuss the questions that follow.

[Read D&C 4:1]

1 "Now behold, a marvelous work is about to come forth among the children of men."

1) In this scripture, a marvelous work is going to happen. Whose work is it? *(Heavenly Father's work.)*

2) What is the marvelous work? (*Heavenly Father's children coming unto Jesus Christ.*)

[Read D&C 4:3]

3 *"Therefore, if ye have desires to serve God ye are called to the work;"*

> 1) Who is called to help Heavenly Father with the marvelous work? (*All of us! If we have a desire, we are called to the work.*)

[Read D&C 4:4]

4 *"For behold the field is white already to harvest; and lo, he that thrusteth in his sickle with his might, the same layeth up in store that he perisheth not, but bringeth salvation to his soul;"*

> 1) What does it mean when it says the "field is white, already to harvest?" (*It means that there are lots of people who are ready to receive Jesus Christ and come unto Him.*)
>
> 2) What does it mean to thrust in your sickle with all your might? (*It means working really hard when we are doing God's work.*)

For a fun way to clean up, you could invite the children to "gather" the remaining wheat kernels on the towel for you!

ACTIVITY PAGES:

[Pass out the Coloring Page]

Invite the children to color the scene from the video. Read the scripture together at the top of the page. Use this opportunity to talk about doing God's work and helping others to come unto Jesus Christ.

♡ TESTIMONY:

Bear testimony of the truths found in the scriptures.

This page intentionally left blank.

"For behold the field is white already to harvest; and lo, he that thrusteth in his sickle with his might, the same layeth up in store that he perisheth not, but bringeth salvation to his soul."

-D&C 4:4

This page intentionally left blank.

Week 6: Feb 3 - 9

 D&C 6-9

 TOPIC | The Spirit of Revelation

♫ **OPENING SONG** "The Holy Ghost"

🗒 **PREPARATION:**

You will need a soft object to throw gently, like a stuffed animal or a soft ball.

💬 **INTRODUCTION:**

Ask for a volunteer. Hand the stuffed animal or soft ball to the volunteer, and then step back a short distance. Ask them to throw the object to you and hold out your hands as if you are going to catch it. When the object comes your direction, hold your arms perfectly still and let the object bounce off of you and land on the floor.

Now discuss the following questions:

1) Did you give the object to me when I asked you to? (*Yes.*)

2) But do I have it now? (*No, it's on the floor!*)

3) Why don't I have it? (*You didn't catch it!*)

4) If you throw something to me, what do I need to do to receive it? (*Catch it with your hands.*)

5) If you tell me something with words, what do I need to do to receive it? (*Listen with your ears.*)

6) If you show me a drawing you made for me, what do I need to do to receive it? (*Look at it with your eyes.*)

Explain: Heavenly Father sends us the Holy Ghost to give us a testimony, to teach us, and to comfort us! But, we must receive the Holy Ghost! We can't hold the Holy Ghost with our arms. And we can't see the Holy Ghost with our eyes. And we can't hear the Holy Ghost with our ears. Instead, we receive the Holy Ghost in our mind (invite the children to point to their minds) and in our hearts (invite the children to point to their hearts).

▶ VIDEO:

Say: "Now we are going to watch a video about radio waves! See if you can tell why radio waves are like the Holy Ghost!"

[Watch Video: "Tuning In To The Holy Ghost | Animated Scripture Lesson for Kids"]

Discuss the following questions after watching the video:

1) Why are radio waves like the Holy Ghost? (Because we can't see the radio waves with our eyes and we can't hear them with our ears.)

2) If we can't see the radio waves and we can't hear them, are they still there? (Yes.)

3) If we want to hear the radio waves, what do we need? (A receiver.)

4) If we want to feel the Holy Ghost, what is the receiver? (Our mind and our heart.)

5) What happens if the radio receiver is not tuned to the right channel? (You won't be able to hear the music.)

6) How can we tune our heart to the Holy Ghost? (By following Jesus Christ and trying to keep the commandments.)

📖 SCRIPTURE:

Read the following scriptures and discuss the questions that follow.

[Doctrine and Covenants 8:2]

2 Yea, behold, I will tell you in your mind and in your heart, by the Holy Ghost, which shall come upon you and which shall dwell in your heart.

1) How will the Holy Ghost tell us things? *(In our mind and in our heart.)*

2) What does "dwell" mean? *(It means to stay somewhere for a long time.)*

3) Where will the Holy Ghost dwell? *(In our heart.)*

[John 14:16]

16 And I will pray the Father, and he shall give you another Comforter, that he may abide with you for ever;

1) Who is speaking in these verses? *(Jesus.)*

2) What is the "Comforter?" *(The Holy Ghost.)*

3) Who sends the Comforter to us? *(Heavenly Father.)*

[John 14:17]

17 Even the Spirit of truth; whom the world cannot receive, because it seeth him not, neither knoweth him: but ye know him; for he dwelleth with you, and shall be in you.

1) Did the world receive the Holy Ghost? *(No. Because they couldn't see the Holy Ghost with their eyes and they didn't know He was there.)*

2) How can we receive the Holy Ghost? *(In our mind and in our heart, and by following Jesus Christ and trying to keep the commandments.)*

3) Who will dwell with us? *(The Holy Ghost will dwell with us.)*

 ## ACTIVITY PAGES:

[Pass out the activity page]

Invite the children to color the radio receiver and to assemble it so that they can "tune in" to the Holy Ghost. Use this time to talk about what we can do to tune our hearts to the Holy Ghost so that the Holy Ghost can dwell in our hearts!

♡ TESTIMONY:

Bear testimony of the truths found in the scriptures.

This page intentionally left blank.

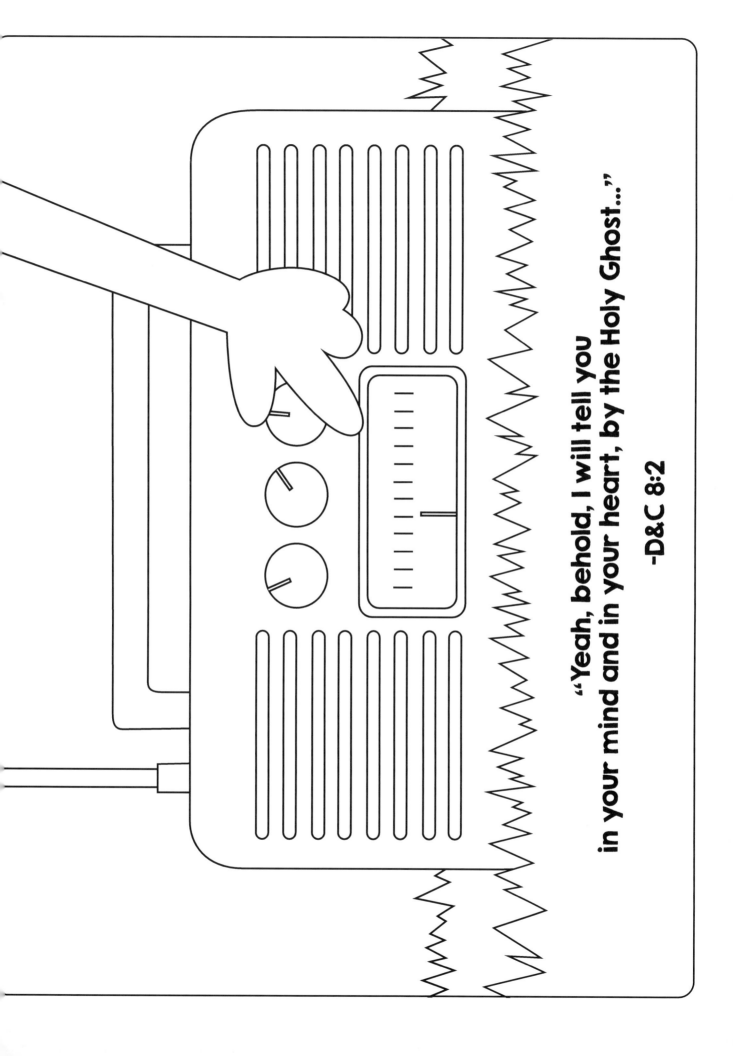

"Yeah, behold, I will tell you in your mind and in your heart, by the Holy Ghost..."

-D&C 8:2

This page intentionally left blank.

Week 7: Feb 10 - 16

 D&C 10-11

 TOPIC | That You May Come Off Conqueror

 OPENING SONG "Did You Think to Pray?"

✎ PREPARATION:

You will need a large bowl or a small cardboard box, a small stick, a string, and a piece of cheese (or any other treat a mouse would like!). Set up a "mouse trap" before the lesson. Tie the string to the stick. Turn the bowl (or box) upside down and use the stick to prop up one side of the bowl. Place the cheese under the bowl.

💬 INTRODUCTION:

Invite the children to inspect the "mouse trap." Tell them to look for the "bait" and to think about how it works. After they have had a chance to explore the trap, explain the following:

Heavenly Father wants us to be happy, but Satan wants to destroy our happiness and ruin Heavenly Father's plan. Satan uses temptations to try to do this.

A temptation is when we see something we want, but we know it is not good for us. It's kind of like a trap! All of us have temptations, and it's not bad to have a temptation. Even Jesus Christ was tempted!

The most important thing is what we do when we face a temptation!

1) Do you think a mouse will be tempted by this cheese? *(Yes.)*

2) What will happen if the mouse resists the temptation and walks away? *(The mouse will be safe from the trap.)*

3) What will happen if the mouse does not resist the temptation and the mouse tries to get the cheese? *(The mouse will be caught in the trap.)*

Now pull the string to demonstrate how the trap works.

VIDEO:

Say: "Now we are going to watch a video about resisting temptations. Heavenly Father told us in the scriptures what we should do to resist temptations. When you are watching this video, see if you can remember what Heavenly Father told us to do to get away from temptations.

[Watch Video: "The Sneaky Bunny | Ainmated Scripture Lesson for Kids"]

Discuss the following questions after watching the video:

1) Was the girl able to get away from the bunny by herself? *(No.)*

2) What did she do when the bunny wouldn't leave her alone and she was really sad? *(She called out to her father.)*

3) What does Heavenly Father tell us we should do to get away from temptations? *(Pray always!)*

SCRIPTURE:

Read the following scriptures and discuss the questions that follow.

[Doctrine and Covenants 10:5]

5 Pray always, that you may come off conqueror; yea, that you may conquer Satan, and that you may escape the hands of the servants of Satan that do uphold his work.

1) What does this scripture tell us we should do to escape and conquer Satan's temptations? *(Pray always.)*

[3 Nephi 18:18]

18 Behold, verily, verily, I say unto you, ye must watch and pray always lest ye enter into temptation; for Satan desireth to have you, that he may sift you as wheat.

1) What does this scripture tell us we should do to escape temptations? *(Watch and pray always.)*

[D&C 20:33]

33 Therefore let the church take heed and pray always, lest they fall into temptation;

1) What does this scripture tell us we should do to escape temptations? *(Take heed and pray always.)*

 ## ACTIVITY PAGES:

[Pass out the Coloring Page]

Invite the children to color the scene from the video. Read the scripture that is on the coloring page with the children. Use this time to talk about praying always to resist temptations.

♡ TESTIMONY:

Bear testimony of the truths found in the scriptures.

This page intentionally left blank.

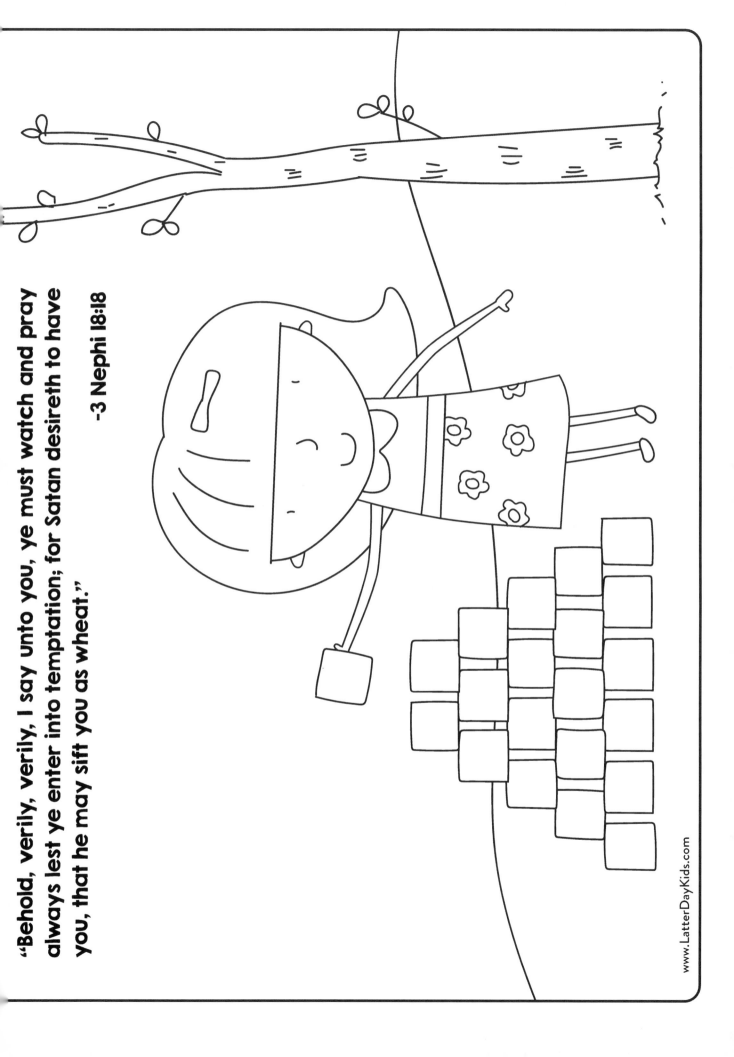

"Behold, verily, verily, I say unto you, ye must watch and pray always lest ye enter into temptation; for Satan desireth to have you, that he may sift you as wheat."

-3 Nephi 18:18

www.LatterDayKids.com

This page intentionally left blank.

Week 8: Feb 17 - 23

 D&C 12-17; JOSEPH SMITH-HISTORY 1:22-75

 TOPIC | Priesthood Keys

 OPENING SONG "Baptism"

 **PREPARATION:**

You will need three keys! Choose three different keys that go to different things. (Car keys, house keys, etc.). Separate them from your keychain so that they can be passed around separately. You will also need three small pieces of paper and a pencil for each child.

💬 INTRODUCTION ACTIVITY:

Pass out a pencil and three pieces of paper to each child. Explain that this is a silent activity. Pass around each key, one at a time. Tell the children to inspect the key carefully and try to figure out what the key is for. When they are ready to guess, tell them to silently draw a picture of what they think the key might be for. (One drawing per paper.)

After completing the activity, reveal the correct answers and see who was able to guess correctly!

Now discuss the following questions:

1) What was this key for? (*Hold up one of the keys and discuss.*)

2) Will this key work for anything else? (*No.*)

3) What was this key for? (*Hold up another key and discuss.*)

4) Will this key work for anything else? (*No.*)

5) What was this key for? (*Hold up the last key and discuss.*)

6) Will this key work for anything else? (*No.*)

7) What happens if we don't have the right keys? (*We can't do those things.*)

Explain:

Today we are going to learn about priesthood keys. Priesthood is the name for God's power. When Heavenly Father gives the priesthood to someone, it's kind of like giving them keys. If they don't have the right priesthood keys, then they can't do those things.

▶️ VIDEO:

Say: "Now we are going to watch a video about a king who gives some keys to his servants. See if you can remember what keys the king gives to the servants."

[Watch Video: "The Castle and the Keys | A Story About Priesthood Keys"]

Discuss the following questions after watching the video:

1) Do you remember what keys the king gave to his servants? (*The watchman had the key to the tower, the gardener had the key to the garden, and the guard had the key to the castle gate.*)

2) Who did the servants get the keys from? (*From the king.*)

3) Did each of the servants get all the keys? (*No, they only got the keys they needed to do what the king asked them to do.*)

4) Can you remember some of the priesthood keys from the video? (*The keys for baptism, administering the sacrament, and giving the Gift of the Holy Ghost.*)

5) Who do we get priesthood keys from? (*From Heavenly Father.*)

📖 SCRIPTURE:

Read the following scriptures and discuss the questions that follow.

[Doctrine and Covenants 13:1]

1 Upon you my fellow servants, in the name of Messiah I confer the Priesthood of Aaron, which holds the keys of the ministering of angels, and of the gospel of repentance, and of baptism by immersion for the remission of sins;

1) Who is receiving priesthood keys in this verse? *(Joseph Smith and Oliver Cowdery.)*

2) What are some of the priesthood keys they received? *(The keys of the ministering of angels, the gospel of repentance, and of baptism.)*

3) Who did they get the keys from? *(Heavenly Father, through John the Baptist.)*

[3 Nephi 11:21-22]

21 And the Lord said unto him: I give unto you power that ye shall baptize this people when I am again ascended into heaven.

22 And again the Lord called others, and said unto them likewise; and he gave unto them power to baptize...

1) Who is receiving priesthood keys in this verse? *(Jesus Christ's disciples that He called among the Nephites.)*

2) What priesthood keys did they receive? *(The keys of baptism.)*

3) Who did they get the keys from? *(Jesus Christ.)*

ACTIVITY PAGES:

[Pass out the Coloring Pages]

Invite the children to draw the symbols for the corresponding priesthood keys. Use this time to talk about priesthood power and priesthood keys.

♡ TESTIMONY:

Bear testimony of the truths found in the scriptures.

This page intentionally left blank.

Keys of the Priesthood

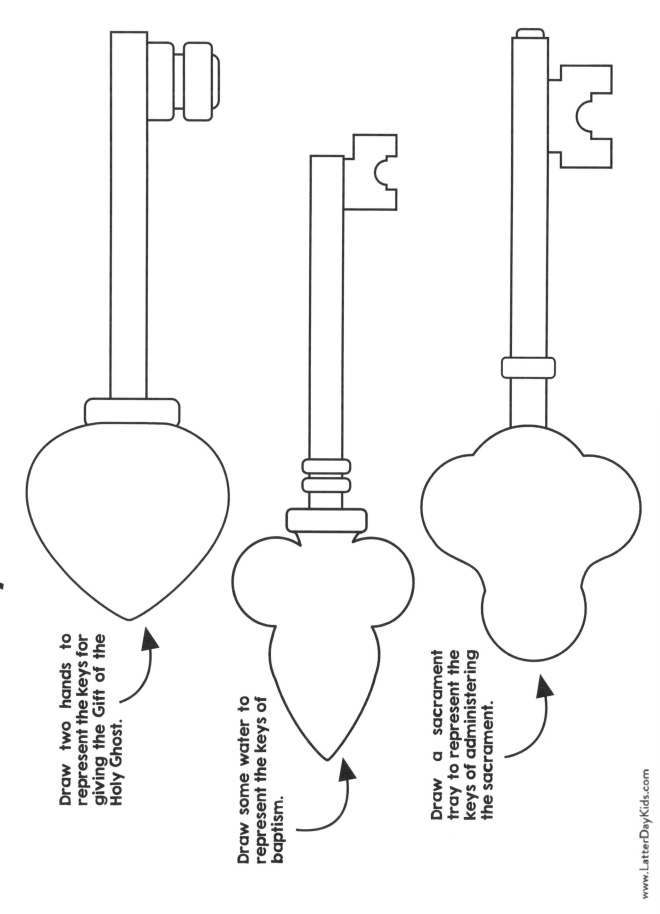

Draw two hands to represent the keys for giving the Gift of the Holy Ghost.

Draw some water to represent the keys of baptism.

Draw a sacrament tray to represent the keys of administering the sacrament.

This page intentionally left blank.

LATTER DAY KIDS

Week 9: Feb 24 - Mar 2

 D&C 18

 TOPIC | The Worth of Souls is Great

 OPENING SONG "My Heavenly Father Loves Me"

PREPARATION:

You will need a fresh dollar bill that is in relatively good shape (or some other type of paper currency), and you will need an individual photo of each person who is present for the lesson. If you don't have a photo of each person, you could also write individual names on small pieces of paper.

INTRODUCTION ACTIVITY:

Hold up the dollar and discuss the following questions:

1) What is this? (*A dollar bill.*)

2) How much is it worth? (*One dollar.*)

3) What can you buy with this dollar? (*Discuss things that the children would like to buy with the dollar.*)

4) Do you want it? (*Yes!*)

Now crumple up the dollar bill, drop it on the floor, kick it around, step on it, etc. Leave it on the floor (still crumpled up), and ask the following questions.

1) Now how much is this dollar worth? (*It is still worth one dollar!*)

2) Can you still buy things with it? (*You can still buy all the same things!*)

55

3) Is this dollar still valuable? *(Yes!)*

4) Do you still want this dollar? *(Yes!)*

Now hold up the individual photos of each person present and explain the following:

Today, we are going to learn about the worth of a soul. Just like the dollar was always valuable to you, you will always be valuable to Heavenly Father! He knows each of you. He knows your names. You are so precious to Him! He always wants you and He always loves you!

VIDEO:

Say: *"Now we are going to watch a video about a girl who sees thousands of starfish washed up on the beach. Let's see what the girl does when she finds them."*

[Watch Video: "The Starfish | Animated Scripture Lesson for Kids"]

Discuss the following questions after watching the video:

1) What did the girl do when she found all the starfish in the sand? *(She was bringing the starfish back to the water.)*

2) Could she help all the starfish? *(No, there were too many for her to help all of them.)*

3) Why did she keep going? Why didn't she give up? *(Because she cared about each individual starfish.)*

4) Do you think Heavenly Father loves all of us? *(Yes!)*

5) Do you think Heavenly Father will ever give up on us or forget about any of us? *(No!)*

6) Why not? *(Because he loves each one of us.)*

SCRIPTURE:

Read the following scriptures and discuss the questions that follow.

[Doctrine and Covenants 18:10-11]

10 Remember the worth of souls is great in the sight of God;

11 For, behold, the Lord your Redeemer suffered death in the flesh; wherefore he suffered the pain of all men, that all men might repent and come unto him.

    1) What does this scripture tell us to remember? *(That our souls are of great worth to God.)*

    2) What did Heavenly Father do that proves how much we are worth to Him? *(He sent His Son Jesus Christ to redeem us.)*

[Doctrine and Covenants 18:13, 16]

13 And how great is his joy in the soul that repenteth!

16 And now, if your joy will be great with one soul that you have brought unto me into the kingdom of my Father, how great will be your joy if you should bring many souls unto me!

    1) What can bring great joy to Heavenly Father? *(He has great joy when a soul repents!)*

    2) How will we feel if we bring a soul to Heavenly Father? *(We will feel great joy!)*

    3) How will we feel if we bring many souls to Heavenly Father? *(We will feel even greater joy!)*

[Doctrine and Covenants 15:6]

6 And now, behold, I say unto you, that the thing which will be of the most worth unto you will be to declare repentance unto this people, that you may bring souls unto me, that you may rest with them in the kingdom of my Father. Amen.

    1) This is a revelation from the Lord to John Whitmer. What did the Lord say John Whitemer could do that would be the most worth? *(Declare repentance and bring souls to Jesus Christ!)*

ACTIVITY PAGES:

[Pass out the Coloring Pages]

Invite the children to color all of the different starfish! Use this as an opportunity to talk about the worth of souls and how we can help bring souls to Heavenly Father.

♡ TESTIMONY:

Bear testimony of the truths found in the scriptures.

This page intentionally left blank.

"REMEMBER THE WORTH OF SOULS IS GREAT IN THE SIGHT OF GOD..."

This page intentionally left blank.

LATTER DAY KIDS

Week 10: Mar 3 - 9

 D&C 19

 TOPIC | The Atonement of Jesus Christ

OPENING SONG "Did Jesus Really Live Again?"

✐ PREPARATION:

Gather some seeds to use as a prop (*something familiar to the children would be ideal*). If you don't have any seeds, you can simply cut out small seed shapes from a piece of paper. Also prepare a small container with some dirt or soil inside (*for "planting" the seeds*).

💬 INTRODUCTION:

Give a seed to each child, then discuss the following questions:

1) What is this that you are holding? (*A seed.*)
2) What can this seed become? (*A plant.*)
3) What has to happen in order for the seed to become a plant? (*Planted in the earth, water, sunlight, etc.*)
4) When the plant starts to grow, what happens to the seed? Will the seed still be there? (*No, the seed won't be there any more - it becomes the plant!*)

Explain that "sacrifice" means to give up something valuable for something else that you want more. If we want to grow a plant, we have to give up the seed.

Ask the children to "plant" their seeds in the small container of dirt. As they do this, explain: "If we want the plant to grow, we must be willing to give up the seed. This is what sacrifice means."

▶ VIDEO:

Say: "We are going to watch a video about Jesus Christ, and the sacrifice that He made for all of us. See if you can tell what Jesus had to sacrifice, and why He was willing to make that sacrifice.

[Watch Video: "The Atonement of Jesus Christ | Animated Scripture Lesson for Kids"]

Discuss the following questions after watching the video:

1) What does it mean to sacrifice something? *(Discuss.)*

2) What sacrifice did Jesus Christ make? *(He suffered pain and sorrow, and He gave up His life.)*

3) What sacrifice did Heavenly Father make? *(He sacrificed His Only Begotten Son.)*

4) What blessings do we receive because of Jesus Christ's sacrifice? *(Resurrection, cleansed from our sins, live with Heavenly Parents again.)*

5) Why did Heavenly Father and Jesus Christ make this sacrifice? *(Because they love us!)*

SCRIPTURE:

Read the scriptures below and discuss the questions that follow.

[Read the last part of Mosiah 4:2]

"O have mercy, and apply the atoning blood of Christ that we may receive forgiveness of our sins, and our hearts may be purified; for we believe in Jesus Christ, the Son of God, who created heaven and earth, and all things; who shall come down among the children of men."

1) Why did these people ask for mercy from the Lord? *(Because they wanted to be forgiven of their sins.)*

2) What does the "atoning blood of Jesus Christ" mean? *(It means the sacrifice that Jesus Christ made for us.)*

[Mosiah 4:8]

"And this is the means whereby salvation cometh. And there is none other salvation save this which hath been spoken of; neither are there any conditions whereby man can be saved except the conditions which I have told you."

    1)   How is it possible for the Heavenly Father to have mercy on us and to make us clean and pure? (*Because of the sacrifice that Jesus Christ made.*)

    2)   Is there any other way for us to be forgiven of our sins and to have salvation? (*No, only through the atonement of Jesus Christ.*)

    2)   Is there any other way for us to be resurrected? (*No, only through the atonement of Jesus Christ.*)

[D&C 19:16]

"For behold, I, God, have suffered these things for all, that they might not suffer if they would repent..."

    1)   What did the Lord suffer for all of us? (*He took our sins upon Himself.*)

    2)   What do we need to do in order to recieve God's Atonement? (*We must repent.*)

✎ ACTIVITY:

[Pass out activity pages]

Option 1: Color and assemble the scene with the sliding tabs (*so that Jesus can move up and down, and the stone can move from side to side*).

Option 2: Color the coloring page.

Use this time to talk about the blessings of the Atonement of Jesus Christ.

♡ TESTIMONY:

Bear testimony of the truths found in the scriptures.

This page intentionally left blank.

This page intentionally left blank.

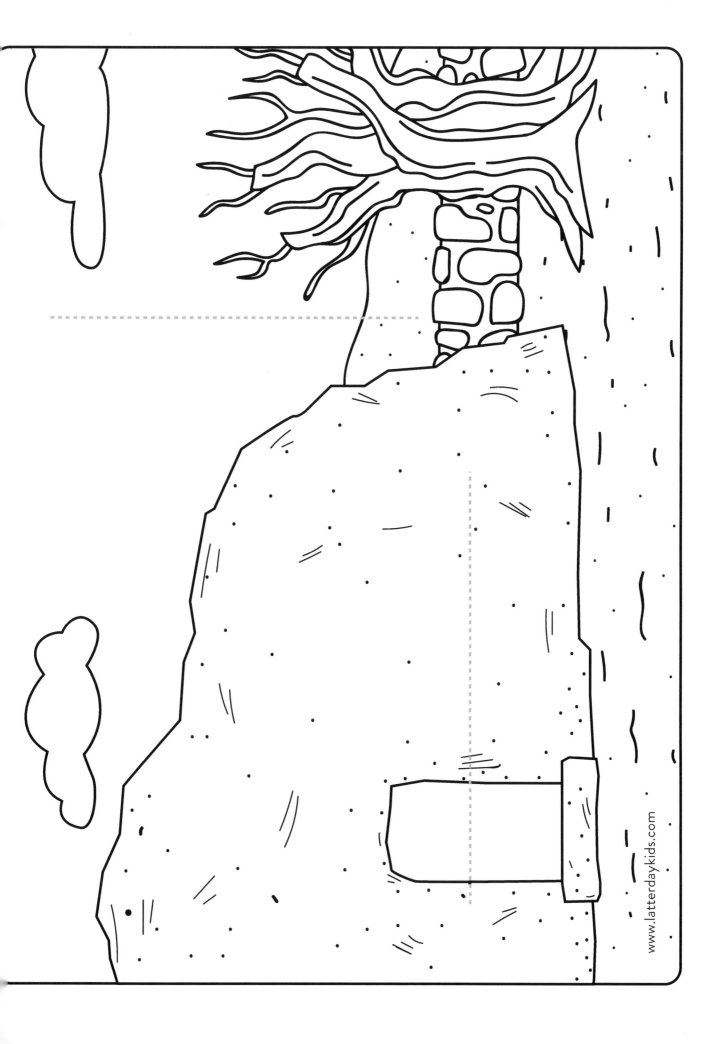

This page intentionally left blank.

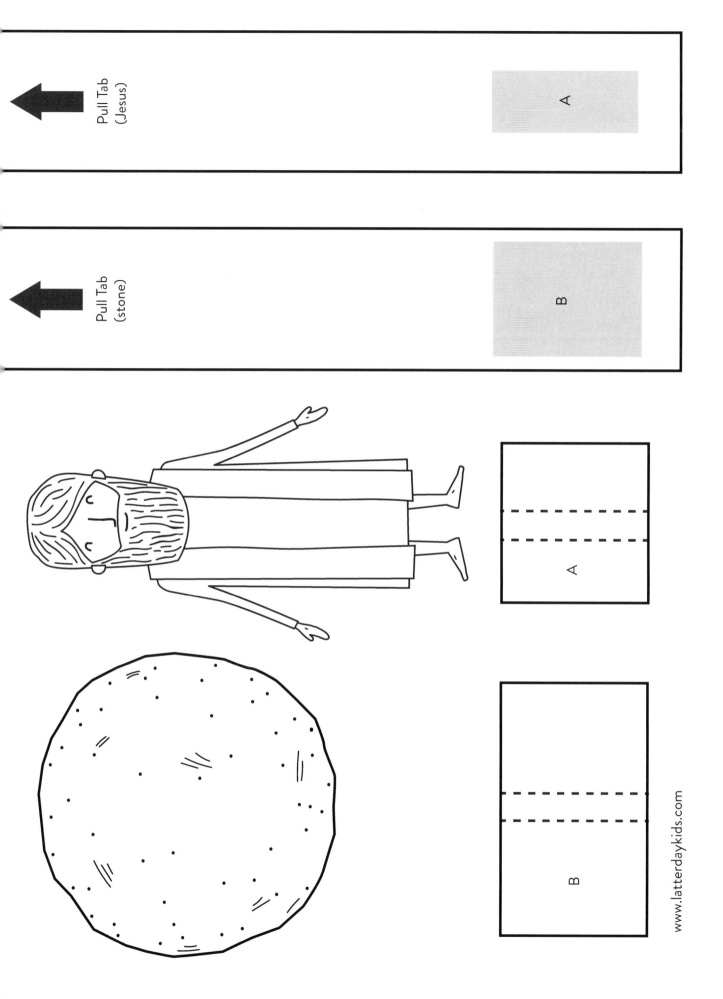

Pull Tab
(Jesus)

A

Pull Tab
(stone)

B

A

B

www.latterdaykids.com

This page intentionally left blank.

LATTER DAY
KIDS

Week 11: Mar 10 - 16

 D&C 20-22

 TOPIC | The Restoration

 OPENING SONG "The Church of Jesus Christ"

📝 **PREPARATION:**

You will need a small bowl, one cup of vinegar, 1 teaspoon of salt, a towel, and several old pennies (darkened and faded).

💬 **INTRODUCTION ACTIVITY:**

Place the bowl on the towel. Pour the vinegar into the bowl and add the salt. Stir until the salt dissolves in the liquid. Pass around the pennies so that the children can inspect them closely and see how dark and old-looking they are. Now ask them the following questions:

1) Did these pennies always look this way? (*No.*)

2) How did they look when they were new? (*They were clean and shiny.*)

Now, say: "We are going to see if we can restore these pennies. If we can restore them, they will look like they did before, when they were new."

Invite the children to place the pennies in the bowl (inside the vinegar and salt solution.) Let the pennies soak for about 60 seconds and allow the children to watch. After 60 seconds, take the pennies out of the vinegar and dry them off on the towel. Allow the children to inspect the pennies and see if any of them were "restored."

Now explain the following:

When Jesus Christ lived on the earth, He formed His church and He gave His apostles priesthood authority. But later, the church started to change, and God took the priesthood authority away from the church. The church wasn't the same any more, and Christ's church wasn't on the earth for many years. It needed to be restored

▶ VIDEO:

Say: "Now we are going to watch a video about an old bicycle. Let's watch and see if anyone will restore the bicycle."

[Watch Video: "The Old Bicycle | Animated Scripture Lesson for Kids"]

Discuss the following questions after watching the video:

1) Did someone restore the bicycle? (*Yes! The boy restored the bicycle!*)

2) What does it mean to restore something? (*It means to bring something back the way it was before.*)

3) What happened after Jesus Christ formed His church on the earth? (*It changed and the priesthood authority was taken away.*)

4) Who restored Jesus Christ's Church? (*God called Joseph Smith to restore Jesus Christ's church.*)

📖 SCRIPTURE:

Read the following scriptures and discuss the questions that follow.

[Doctrine and Covenants 20:1]

1 The rise of the Church of Christ in these last days, being one thousand eight hundred and thirty years since the coming of our Lord and Savior Jesus Christ in the flesh...

1) What is being restored in this verse? (*The Church of Christ.*)

2) What year was the Church of Christ restored? (*1830.*)

[Doctrine and Covenants 127:8]

8 For I am about to restore many things to the earth, pertaining to the priesthood, saith the Lord of Hosts.

    1) Who is speaking in this verse? *(The Lord.)*

    2) What did the Lord say He was about to do? *(Restore many things to the earth pertaining to the priesthood.)*

[Doctrine and Covenants 15:6]

45 For I have conferred upon you the keys and power of the priesthood, wherein I restore all things, and make known unto you all things in due time.

    1) Who is the Lord speaking to in this verse? *(To Joseph Smith.)*

    2) What is being restored in this verse? *(The keys and power of the priesthood, and all things in due time.*

ACTIVITY PAGES:

[Pass out the Coloring Pages]

Invite the children to "restore" the bicycle by following the instructions and drawing the necessary repairs! Use this time to talk about the restoration of the Church of Jesus Christ through the prophet Joseph Smith.

♡ TESTIMONY:

Bear testimony of the truths found in the scriptures.

This page intentionally left blank.

Can you restore this bicycle? First, pump up the tires! Then, draw the missing spokes inside the wheels. Next, add a new chain! Last of all, give the bike a fresh coat of paint!

"I am the Lord thy God, and I gave unto thee, my servant Joseph, an appointment, and restore all things. For I have conferred upon you the keys and power of the priesthood, wherein I restore all things and make known unto you all things in due time."

-D&C 132:40, 45

www.LatterDayKids.com

This page intentionally left blank.

LATTER DAY KIDS

Week 12: Mar 17 - 23

 D&C 23-26

 TOPIC | The Song of the Heart

🎵 **OPENING SONG** "A Child's Prayer"

🗒 **PREPARATION:**

You will need a whiteboard (or a large sheet of paper or posterboard) and a timer.

💬 **INTRODUCTION ACTIVITY:**

Invite the children to think of things that make Heavenly Father and Jesus Christ happy. Tell the children that the goal is to think of as many things as they can in one minute. Draw a happy face on the whiteboard (or on the large sheet of paper) for each answer the children come up with. Set the timer for one minute and begin! When the time runs out, count how many things the children were able to think of.

Explain: Today's lesson is about something that makes Heavenly Father and Jesus Christ really happy! Tell the children you are going to read a scripture to them, and to see if they can guess what it is!

(Explain that the Lord is speaking in this verse)

"For my soul delighteth in the song of the heart." -D&C 25:12

Now discuss the following questions:

   1) Do you know what "delight" means? (*A feeling of great happiness or pleasure.*)

2) What is it that delights the Lord? *(The song of the heart.)*

VIDEO:

Say: "Now we are going to watch three little birds who like to sing! Let's watch and see if anyone is delighted when they hear the birds singing!"

[Watch Video: "The Song Of The Heart | Animated Scripture Lesson for Kids"]

Discuss the following questions after watching the video:

1) Who got to hear the birds singing? *(The woodpecker, the beavers, and the turtle.)*

2) Do you think the other animals were delighted when they heard the singing? *(Yes!)*

3) How did you know they were delighted? *(They were dancing and joining in with the singing!)*

4) Do you think Jesus is delighted when you sing? *(Discuss.)*

5) What are your favorite things to sing about? *(Discuss.)*

SCRIPTURE:

Read the following scriptures and discuss the questions that follow.

[Doctrine and Covenants 25:11]

11 And it shall be given thee, also, to make a selection of sacred hymns, as it shall be given thee, which is pleasing unto me, to be had in my church.

1) Do you know who the Lord is talking to in this verse? *(Emma Smith.)*

2) What does the Lord ask Emma to do? *(To choose a songs to be sung in church.)*

3) Why do you think the Lord wanted Emma to do this? *(Discuss.)*

[Ephesians 5:19]

19 ...Speaking to yourselves in psalms and hymns and spiritual songs, singing and making melody in your heart to the Lord;

1) Do you know who is speaking in this verse? (*The apostle Paul.*)

2) Do you know who the apostle Paul is speaking to? (*To the members of the church.*)

3) What did the Apostle Paul teach the members of the church to do? (*To speak to each other in hymns and songs, and to sing to the Lord.*)

[Ether 6:9]

9 And they did sing praises unto the Lord; yea, the brother of Jared did sing praises unto the Lord, and he did thank and praise the Lord all the day long; and when the night came, they did not cease to praise the Lord.

1) Do you know who this verse is talking about? (*It's when the Jaredites were traveling across the ocean in the barges.*)

2) Who were they singing to while they were in the barges? (*They were singing to the Lord.*)

3) How long did they sing and give thanks to the Lord? (*All day long.*)

ACTIVITY PAGES:

[Pass out the Coloring Pages]

Invite the children to color the scenes from the video and to fill in the bubbles with the things that they want to sing about. Use this time to talk about the singing and how it delights Heavenly Father and Jesus Christ when we sing songs of the heart.

♡ TESTIMONY:

Bear testimony of the truths found in the scriptures.

This page intentionally left blank.

"For my soul delighteth in the song of the heart..."
-D&C 25:11

Directions: Color the birds. Next, think of some things that you would like to sing to the Lord about! Draw pictures of those things in the word bubbles.

This page intentionally left blank.

LATTER DAY KIDS

Week 13: Mar 24-30

 D&C 27-28

💡 **TOPIC** | All Things Must Be Done In Wisdom and Order

🎵 **OPENING SONG** "We Thank Thee O God for a Prophet"

📝 **PREPARATION:**

You will need 10 toys of various sizes (the children will be putting them in order from largest to smallest).

💬 **INTRODUCTION ACTIVITY:**

Place the toys randomly on the floor in a messy pile. Explain to the children that the toys are out of order. Invite the children to reposition the toys and put them in order in a straight row, largest to smallest. After the children have completed the activity, ask them to return to their seats and then discuss the following questions.

1) Were the toys in order at the beginning? (*No.*)

2) Were the toys in order when you were finished? (*Yes.*)

3) Can you think of anything else in your house that is in order? (*Some examples might be clothes organized into drawers, trash in the trash can, dishe s that are stacked, etc.*)

4) Do you think Heavenly Father's house is a house of order? Or a house of confusion? (*A house of order.*)

5) Why do you think Heavenly Father's house is a house of order? (*Discuss.*)

Explain: One of the ways that Heavenly Father keeps His house in order is by calling a prophet to lead his church. If we didn't have a prophet, we would be confused and things would get out of order!

VIDEO:

Say: "Now we are going to watch a video about a pirate ship! Let's see if there is order on the ship, or if there is confusion!"

[Watch Video: "Atlas and the Pirate Ship | Animated Scripture Lesson for Kids"]

Discuss the following questions after watching the video:

1) Was there order on the ship at the beginning? Or was there confusion? (*There was confusion!*)

2) Was there order on the ship at the end? (Yes!)

3) What brought order to the ship? (They all knew who the captain was!)

4) Who does the captain represent? (The prophet.)

5) What do you think would happen if we didn't have a prophet? (Discuss.)

SCRIPTURE:

Read the following scriptures and discuss the questions that follow.

[Doctrine and Covenants 28:13]

13 For all things must be done in order, and by common consent in the church, by the prayer of faith.

1) How does Heavenly Father want things to be done in his church? (*In order and by common consent.*)

[Doctrine and Covenants 132:8]

8 Behold, mine house is a house of order, saith the Lord God, and not a house of confusion.

1) What kind of house is the Lord's house? (*A house of order.*)

2) Is the Lord's house a house of confusion? (*No.*)

3) What did the Apostle Paul teach the members of the church to do? (*To speak to each other in hymns and songs, and to sing to the Lord.*)

[Alma 13:1]

1 ...and I would that ye should remember that the Lord God ordained priests, after his holy order, which was after the order of his Son, to teach these things unto the people.

    1) Were the priests ordained with confusion, or with order? *(With order.)*

    2) What were they ordained to do? *(To teach these things.)*

 ## ACTIVITY PAGES:

[Pass out the Coloring Pages]

Invite the children to color the scene from the video. Use this time to talk about the order of things in Christ's church.

♡ TESTIMONY:

Bear testimony of the truths found in the scriptures.

This page intentionally left blank.

"For all things must be done in order..." -D&C 28:13

www.LatterDayKids.com

This page intentionally left blank.

LATTER DAY
KIDS

Week 14: Mar 31 – Apr 6

 D&C 29

 TOPIC | The Plan of Salvation

🎵 **OPENING SONG** "I Will Follow God's Plan"

✎ **PREPARATION:**

Each person will need a blank piece of paper and something to write or draw with.

💬 **INTRODUCTION ACTIVITY:**

Invite each child to imagine it's going to be their birthday soon and it's time to make a plan! Tell each child to think of 5 things that they would like to do at their imaginary birthday party and to write or draw a picture of each idea on their paper.

After children have had time to think of things they would like to plan, invite children to share their plans with the group.

After this activity, ask the following questions:

1) Why is it important to make a plan for something before it happens? (*To make sure we don't forget anything, it lets everyone know what's going to happen, to make sure we are prepared, etc.*)

2) Can you think of other things that people make plans for? (*A vacation, a class or lesson, building a house, etc.*)

3) Do you think Heavenly Father makes plans? (Discuss.)

4) What do you think Heavenly Father might want to make a plan for? (Discuss.)

▶ VIDEO:

Say: "We are going to watch a video about Heavenly Father's plan for us. See if you can remember three things that He has planned for us."

[Watch Video: "The Plan of Salvation | Animated Scripture Lesson"]

Discuss the following questions after watching the video:

1) Can you remember three things from the video that Heavenly Father has planned for us? (*Discuss.*)

2) Did we have a physical body when we lived with Heavenly Father in the premortal life? (*Only a spirit body.*)

3) What did Heavenly Father plan for us to receive? (*A physical body.*)

4) What happens when our body dies? (*It is buried in the earth.*)

5) What happens to our spirit when we die? (*It goes to the spirit world or to spirit prison.*)

6) What does it mean to be resurrected? (*Our spirit is reunited with our body and we won't die any more.*)

7) What are some things that Heavenly Father planned for Jesus Christ to do? (*Help create the earth, pay the price for our sins, overcome death etc.*)

8) When will we be judged? (*After we are resurrected.*)

9) What has Heavenly Father planned for us after the final judgement? (*That we will live in one of the kingdoms of glory.*)

📖 SCRIPTURE:

Read the verses below and discuss the questions that follow.

[D&C 29:39]

39 And it must needs be that the devil should tempt the children of men, or they could not be agents unto themselves; for if they never should have bitter they could not know the sweet—

1) Why does Heavenly Father plan for us to be tempted? (*So we can learn to make choices and choose good by ourselves.*)

[D&C 29:13]

13 ...and they shall come forth—yea, even the dead which died in me, to receive a crown of righteousness, and to be clothed upon, even as I am, to be with me, that we may be one.

1) What has Heavenly Father planned for us after we die? (*He has planned for us to come forth and be resurrected, and for us to be with Him.*)

[Alma 21:9]

9 Now Aaron began to open the scriptures unto them concerning the coming of Christ, and also concerning the resurrection of the dead, and that there could be no redemption for mankind save it were through the death and sufferings of Christ, and the atonement of his blood.

1) Could there be a resurrection if Jesus Christ wasn't part of the plan? (*No.*)

2) Could we be redeemed if Jesus Christ wasn't part of the plan? (*No.*)

✏️ ACTIVITY PAGES:

[Pass out activity pages]

Invite children to color the image from the video. As they color take to opportunity to talk together about Heavenly Father's Plan of Salvation.

♡ TESTIMONY:

Bear testimony of the truths found in the scriptures.

This page intentionally left blank.

This page intentionally left blank.

LATTER DAY KIDS

Week 15: April 7 - 13

 D&C 30-36

 TOPIC | Letting Go of the Things of the World

 **OPENING SONG** "I Know My Father Lives"

PREPARATION:

You will need a jar and a ball (or some other round object) that is slightly smaller than the opening of the jar.

INTRODUCTION ACTIVITY:

Invite a volunteer to attempt to reach into the jar and remove the ball with their hand. (They should be unable to remove their hand from the jar unless they let go of the ball). Allow other volunteers to try as well.

Once you have finished the activity, discuss the following questions:

1) What happened when you were holding onto the ball? (*You couldn't get your hand out of the jar.*)

2) What did you have to do if you wanted to get your hand out of the jar? (*You had to let go of the ball.*)

3) If you kept holding onto the ball, could you ever get your hand out? (*No. Only if you let go of the ball.*)

4) Can you think of some things that can trap us when we are trying to follow Heavenly Father? (*Discuss things like lying, contention, stealing, being unkind, sin, etc.*)

5) Does Heavenly Father want us to hold on to those things? Or does he want us to let go of them? *(He wants us to let go.)*

▶ VIDEO:

Say: "We are going to watch a video about Layla the Ladybug. Layla wants to fly high in the forest. But she can't fly high until she lets go of some things. See if you can find out what she needs to let go of."

[Watch Video: "Layla the Ladybug | Animated Scripture Lesson for Kids"]

Discuss the following questions after watching the video:

1) What did Layla have to let go of if she wanted to fly high in the sky? *(The rock, the leaves, and the boots.)*

2) Why was Layla holding on to those things? *(She was afraid that the other ladybugs would make fun of her, and she thought those things would make her happy.)*

3) Did those things really make Layla happy? *(No.)*

4) Who knows the best way for Layla to be happy? *(Heavenly Father.)*

5) What did Layla decide to do? *(to let go of the other things and follow Heavenly Father.)*

6) Who knows the best way for all of us to be happy? *(Heavenly Father.)*

SCRIPTURE:

Read the verses below and discuss the questions that follow.

[D&C 30:1]

1 Behold, I say unto you, David, that you have feared man and have not relied on me for strength as you ought.

1) Who is Heavenly Father talking to in this scripture? *(David Whitmer.)*

2) What warning did Heavenly Father give to David Whitmer? *(That he feared man and wasn't relying on God for his strength.)*

3) Are we afraid of what others will think of us sometimes? *(Discuss.)*

4) What would Heavenly Father tell us to do? *(Discuss.)*

[Matthew 6:24]

24 No man can serve two masters: for either he will hate the one, and love the other; or else he will hold to the one, and despise the other. Ye cannot serve God and mammon.

1) What is mammon? *(It means worldly things.)*

2) Who knows the best way for all of us to be happy? Heavenly Father? Or the world? *(Heavenly Father.)*

3) Can we serve God and hold on to worldly things at the same time? *(No.)*

 ## ACTIVITY PAGES:

[Pass out activity pages]

Invite children to color the image from the video as you talk together about letting go of the things of the world to follow Heavenly Father.

♡ TESTIMONY:

Bear testimony of the truths found in the scriptures.

This page intentionally left blank.

"No man can serve two masters: for either he will hate the one, and love the other; or else he will hold to the one, and despise the other. Ye cannot serve God and mammon." -Matthew 6:24

www.latterdaykids.com

This page intentionally left blank.

Week 16: Apr 14 - 20

 EASTER

TOPIC | Easter

♪ **OPENING SONG** "Did Jesus Really Live Again?"

✐ **PREPARATION:**

You will need a cup that is opaque (not see-through), some paper towels, and another clear glass with a small amount of water in it. Before the lesson begins, stack the paper towels together, fold them in half, and then roll them up tightly. Bend the roll into a "C" shape and compress the roll tightly into the bottom of the opaque cup so that it stays in position even when the cup is turned upside down.

💬 INTRODUCTION ACTIVITY:

Hold the glass of water up in front of the group. Explain that this is a glass of real water. Take a small drink to show them it's real. Drink the water until there is only about 1/8 cup left. Now hold up the opaque cup and pour the water into it. Wait for just a moment to allow the water to soak into the paper towels. Now tell the children that when you turn the cup around, no water will come out. Ask them if they believe you. Now, turn the cup upside down. It will appear that the water has vanished!

After this activity, discuss the following questions:

1) Did you see me pour the water into the cup? *(Yes.)*

2) What should have happened when I turned the cup upside down? *(The water should have poured out of the cup.)*

3) Did you believe me when I said no water would pour out of the cup? (Discuss.)

4) Were you surprised when no water poured out of the cup? *(Yes.)*

5) Jesus told many people that He would be resurrected after He died. Do you think His followers believed Him? *(Yes.)*

6) When Jesus was resurrected, do you think some of them were still surprised? *(Yes!)*

Explain the following: Today, we are going to learn about the resurrection of Jesus Christ. His body was in the tomb for three days after He died. When He was resurrected, it was a miracle!

▶ VIDEO:

Say: "We are going to watch a video about a girl named Lily who is going on an Easter egg hunt! See if you can remember what surprises were inside each of the eggs!"

[Watch Video: "The Easter Surprise | Animated Scripture Lesson for Kids"]

Discuss the following questions after watching the video:

1) Can you remember each of the surprises that Lily found in the eggs? *(Jelly beans, marbles, money, a chocolate bunny, and an empty egg!)*

2) What was the reason for the empty egg? What does that make us think about? *(It can remind us of the empty tomb.)*

3) Why was Mary sad when she went to the tomb? *(She thought someone took Jesus Christ's body away.)*

4) Why was the tomb empty? *(Because Jesus was resurrected!)*

5) Do you think Mary was surprised when she saw that Jesus was resurrected? *(Yes!)*

SCRIPTURE:

Read the verses below and discuss the questions that follow.

[John 20:11-12]

But Mary stood without at the sepulchre weeping: and as she wept, she stooped down, and looked into the sepulchre...

    1) Why was Mary weeping? *(Because Jesus' body was gone and she didn't know where it was.)* [John 20:16]

Jesus saith unto her, Mary. She turned herself, and saith unto him, Rabboni; which is to say, Master.

    1) Who spoke to Mary? *(The resurrected Jesus!)*

    2) How do you think Mary felt when she saw Jesus? *(Discuss.)*

    3) How do you think it will feel when we see the people that we love for the first time after they are resurrected? *(Discuss.)*

[Mosiah 15:20]

But behold, the bands of death shall be broken, and the Son reigneth, and hath power over the dead; therefore, he bringeth to pass the resurrection of the dead.

    1) Who has power over death? *(Jesus Christ!)*

    2) Who will be resurrected? *(All of us will be resurrected because of Jesus Christ!)*

ACTIVITY PAGES:

Invite children to color the images from the video. As they color, take the opportunity to talk together about Easter and the resurrection of Jesus Christ.

♡ TESTIMONY:

Bear testimony of the truths found in the scriptures.

This page intentionally left blank.

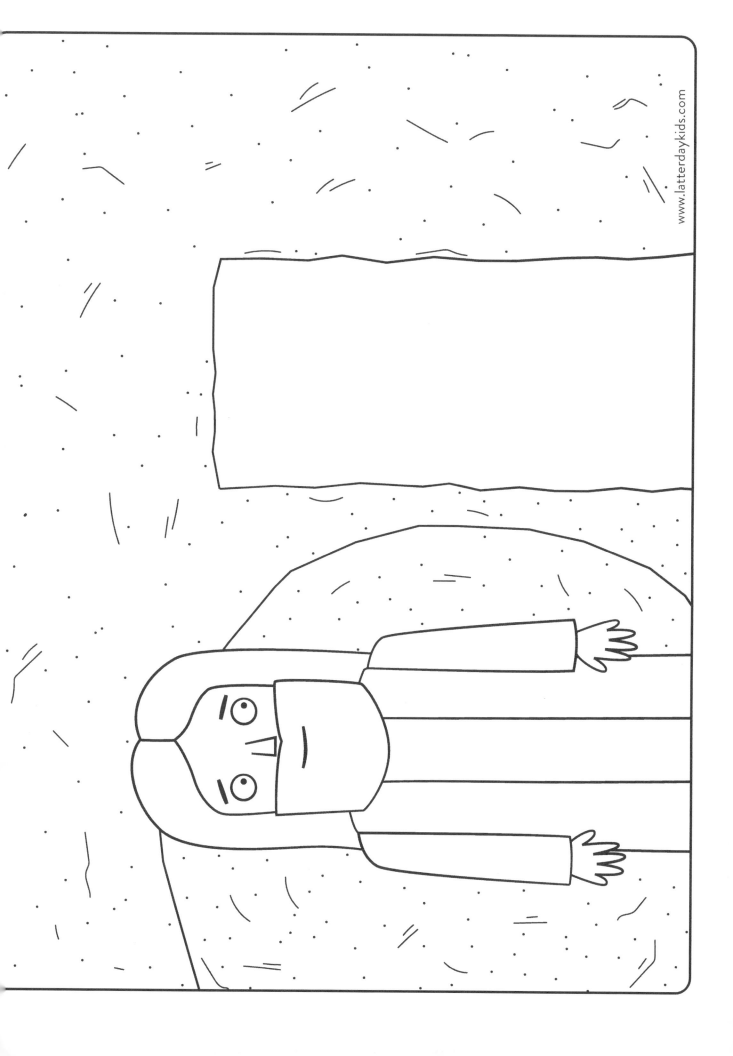

This page intentionally left blank.

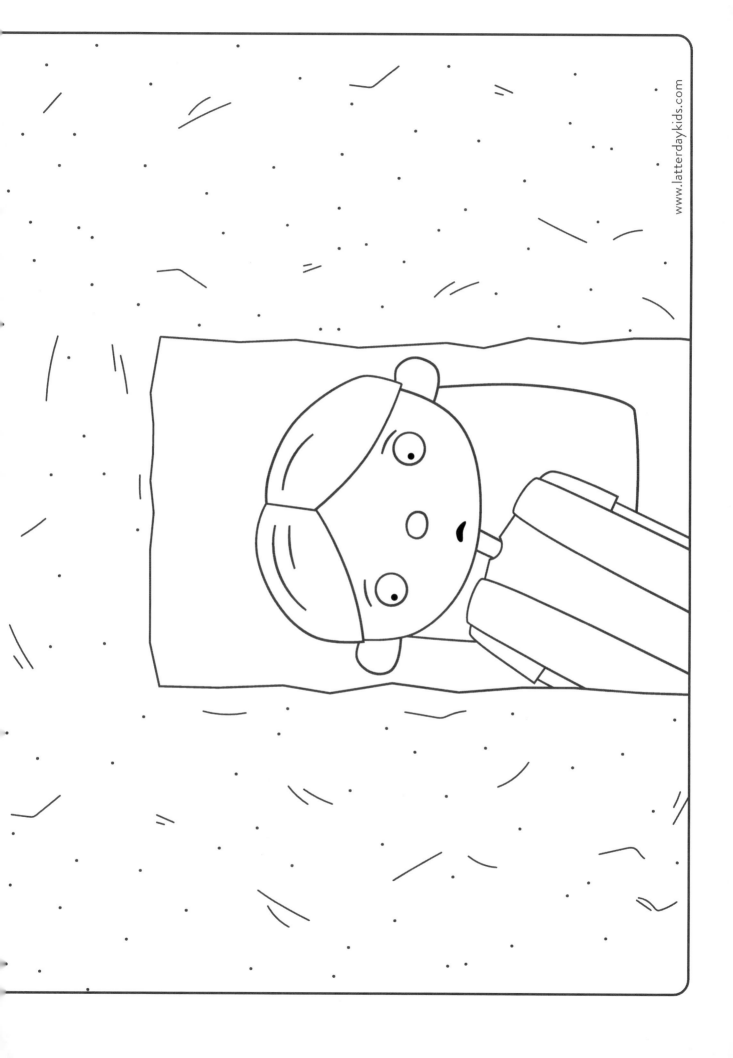

This page intentionally left blank.

Week 17: Apr 21 - 27

 D&C 37-40

 TOPIC | If Ye Are Not One Ye Are Not Mine

♫ **OPENING SONG** "I'll Walk With You"

📝 **PREPARATION:**

You will need a flashlight that can be taken apart into several pieces. Take the flashlight apart before the lesson.

💬 **INTRODUCTION ACTIVITY:**

Place all of the individual pieces of the flashlight on a flat surface where everyone can see them. One by one, ask the children to identify each piece and explain what it is for/what it does.

Example:

The light bulb makes the light.
The battery supplies the power.
The case holds the pieces together.

Once you have talked about each individual part, discuss the following questions:

1) Do you think these pieces can work on their own? Or do you think they need each other? *(They need each other.)*

2) What would happen if the battery tried to be a flashlight all by itself? *(It wouldn't be able to make any light.)*

3) What would happen if the light bulb tried to shine all by itself? *(It wouldn't work.)*

4) Do you think He wants us to be by ourselves? Or do you think He wants us to be together with Him and with our brothers and sisters? *(Discuss.)*

▶ VIDEO:

Say: "We are going to watch a video about a "truck squad!" In the beginning, each truck is alone, and things aren't going very well. Watch and see what the trucks decide to do!

[Watch Video: "The Truck Squad | Animated Scripture Lesson for Kids"]

Discuss the following questions after watching the video:

1) What could the gas truck do? *(It could give gas to the other trucks.)*

2) What could the tire truck do? *(It could give new tires to the other trucks.)*

3) What could the crane truck do? *(It could lift heavy things.)*

4) What could the fire truck do? *(It could put out fires.)*

5) What happened when the trucks were alone? *(They all got stuck!)*

6) What did the trucks decide to do? *(Work together as one.)*

7) Can you think of any bugs or animals that work together as one? *(Bees, ants, etc.)*

8) What are some things you could do to help others and work as one? *(Discuss.)*

SCRIPTURE:

Read the verses below and discuss the questions that follow.

[D&C 38:25]

25 And again I say unto you, let every man esteem his brother as himself.

1) Who is speaking in this verse? *(The Lord is giving instructions to the church.)*

2) What does it mean to "esteem your brother as yourself?" *(Treat others the way you want to be treated.)*

3) How do you want to be treated? *(Discuss.)*

[D&C 38:27]

27 I say unto you, be one; and if ye are not one ye are not mine.

1) What does it mean to be one? *(It means to work together and help each other.)*

2) Who does the Lord command to be one? *(Members of the church.)*

3) What do you think will happen if members of the church don't work together as one? *(Discuss.)*

4) Why do you think He wants us to be one? *(Discuss.)*

5) Do you think Heavenly Father also wants our families to be one? Why? *(Discuss.)*

ACTIVITY PAGES:

[Pass out activity pages]

Invite children to color the trucks from the "Truck Squad!" Read the scripture on the pages. Cut out the trucks and have them "drive" around and help each other!

♡ TESTIMONY:

Bear testimony of the truths found in the scriptures.

This page intentionally left blank.

"I say unto you, be one; and if ye are not one ye are not mine."

-D&C 38:27

This page intentionally left blank.

"I say unto you, be one; and if ye are not one ye are not mine."

-D&C 38:27

This page intentionally left blank.

LATTER DAY KIDS

Week 18: Apr 28 - May 4

 D&C 41-44

 TOPIC | Discipleship

 OPENING SONG "I'm Trying to Be Like Jesus"

PREPARATION:

You will need a blindfold for each person (except one) who will be present at the lesson.

INTRODUCTION ACTIVITY:

Ask for a volunteer to be the "leader" and play "follow the leader." (Invite the leader to do things like walk around the room, sit down, stand up, run in place, etc.) while all of the other participants try to mimic the leader.

Now, pass out the blindfolds to the "followers" and ask everyone to play follow the leader again with the blindfolds on. (This should be much more difficult because the followers cannot see the leader.)

After this activity, discuss the following questions:

1) What happened when you couldn't see the leader? (*It was harder to follow the leader!*)

2) Jesus Christ invited us to follow Him. Do you think we can follow Him if we aren't watching Him? (*Discuss.*)

3) How can we learn about Jesus Christ? (*The scriptures, church, Family Home Evening, prayer.*)

4) If we want to follow Jesus Christ, is it better to learn only a little about Him? Or should we learn a lot about Him? (*A lot!*)

5) Why is it better to learn a lot about Jesus Christ? (*We will be able to follow Him better if we know more about Him.*)

Explain: Today, we are going to learn about the word "Disciple." A disciple of Jesus Christ is someone who learns about Jesus Christ and follows Him.

VIDEO:

Say: "Now we are going to watch a video about a little spider who wanted to follow the master spider! Let's watch and see if the little blue spider learns how to be a disciple!"

[Watch Video: "The Little Blue Spider | A Story About Discipleship"]

Discuss the following questions after watching the video:

1) Did the little blue spider learn how to be a disciple? (*Yes.*)

2) How do you know that the little blue spider was a disciple? (*He learned more about the master spider every day, and he tried to do everything that the master spider did.*)

3) What does it mean to be a disciple of Jesus Christ? (*It means to learn about Jesus Christ and to try to follow Him and be like Him.*)

4) If we want to be a disciple of Jesus Christ, do you think we should learn about Him? (*Yes.*)

5) How can we learn about Jesus Christ? (*The scriptures, church, Family Home Evening, prayer.*)

SCRIPTURE:

Read the verses below and discuss the questions that follow.

[D&C 41:5]

5 *He that receiveth my law and doeth it, the same is my disciple...*

1) Who is speaking in this verse? (*Jesus Christ.*)

2) How can we become His disciple? (*By receiving His law and doing it.*)

3) What will happen if we don't know Jesus Christ's laws? *(It will be harder for us to follow Him.)*

[John 13:34-35]

34 A new commandment I give unto you, That ye love one another; as I have loved you, that ye also love one another.

35 By this shall all men know that ye are my disciples, if ye have love one to another.

    1) What commandment did Jesus give to us in these verses? *(Love one another as Jesus Loves us.)*

    2) How will others know if we are a disciple of Jesus Christ? *(If we love one another the way that Jesus loves us.)*

[Matthew 11:28-29]

28 Come unto me, all ye that labour and are heavy laden, and I will give you rest.

29 Take my yoke upon you, and learn of me...

    1) What is a yoke? *(It is a device that hooks two animals together so they go the same way together.)*

    2) What did Jesus Christ tell us to do in this verse? *(To come unto Him, to take His yoke on us, and learn of Him.)*

    3) Do you think learning of Jesus Christ will help us be a better disciple of Jesus Christ? Why? *(Discuss.)*

ACTIVITY PAGES:

[Pass out activity pages]

Invite children to color the image from the video as you talk together about what it means to be a disciple of Jesus Christ.

♡ TESTIMONY:

Bear testimony of the truths found in the scriptures.

This page intentionally left blank.

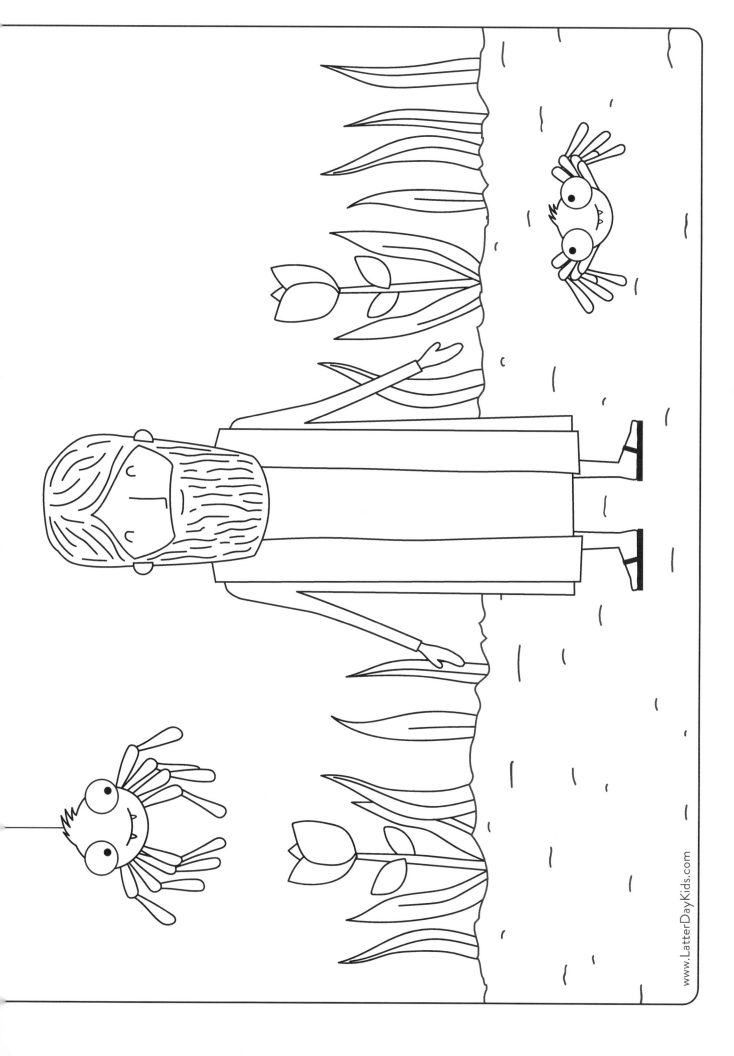

This page intentionally left blank.

LATTER DAY KIDS

Week 19: May 5 - 11

 D&C 45

 TOPIC | Stand in Holy Places

 OPENING SONG "I Love to See the Temple"

PREPARATION:

You will need 5-10 towels, some sheets of blank paper, and a large marker to write on the paper with.

INTRODUCTION ACTIVITY:

Place the towels on the floor to create a pathway of "stepping stones" leading across the room. Leave some space between them so that the children will need to reach slightly to step from one towel to the next.

Invite the children to play the "hot lava" game! The goal is to get from one side of the room to the other without touching the hot lava (the floor)! The towels serve as safe spaces where it is safe to stand!

Once you have completed the activity, discuss the following questions:

1) Did you make it to the other side? (*Yes!*)

2) How did you do it? (*By standing on the safe spaces.*)

3) What would happen if there were no safe spaces? (*They couldn't make it across the room and they would have to go in the lava!*)

4) Do you think your Heavenly Father wants you to make it safely back to Him? (Yes!)

5) What are some safe spaces that Heavenly Father has given us to help us on our journey? *(Discuss things such as scriptures, living prophets, our families, the church, the temple, good friends, prayer, etc.)*

As you talk about each idea, write it on a sheet of paper and place it on one of the towels.

VIDEO:

Say: "We are going to watch a video about a girl who lives near a meadow. Her family needs to cross the river sometimes, but there is no bridge. Watch, and see if you can find out how they can get across the river safely!

[Watch Video: "Stand in Holy Places | Animated Scripture Lesson for Kids"]

Discuss the following questions after watching the video:

1) How did the girl and her family get across the river? *(They stood on the rocks!)*

2) What did the river represent? *(The world and the influence of the world.)*

3) What did the rocks represent? *(Holy places, Heavenly Father, and the Holy Ghost).*

4) Do you think Heavenly Father is strong enough to keep us safe from the influences of the world? *(Yes!)*

5) What do we have to do? *(Stand in holy places.)*

6) What does it mean to stand in holy places? *(To go to places where the Holy Ghost can be, and to do the things that will invite the Holy Ghost to be with us!)*

SCRIPTURE:

Read the verses below and discuss the questions that follow.

[D&C 45:32]

32 But my disciples shall stand in holy places, and shall not be moved..."

1) What is a disciple? *(Someone who follows Jesus Christ.)*

2) What does the Lord say His disciples should do? *(Stand in holy places.)*

3) What are some things we can do to stand in holy places and not be moved? *(Discuss.)*

[Psalms 24:3-4]

3 Who shall ascend into the hill of the Lord? or who shall stand in his holy place?

4 He that hath clean hands, and a pure heart; who hath not lifted up his soul unto vanity, nor sworn deceitfully.

    1) What do you think it means to have clean hands? *(Discuss.)*

    2) What do you think it means to have a pure heart? *(Discuss.)*

    3) How will standing in Holy places help us? *(Discuss.)*

 ## ACTIVITY PAGES:

[Pass out activity pages]

Invite children to color the scene from the video. Read the scripture together and discuss what you can do to "stand in holy places."

♡ TESTIMONY:

Bear testimony of the truths found in the scriptures.

This page intentionally left blank.

"But my disciples shall astand in holy places, and shall not be moved..."

-D&C 45:32

This page intentionally left blank.

Week 20: May 12 - 18

 D&C 46-48

 TOPIC | Spiritual Gifts

OPENING SONG "I Am A Child of God"

PREPARATION:

You will need 5-10 coins (quarters would work well). Before the lesson, hide the quarters around the room in places where they are visible, but still somewhat hidden.

INTRODUCTION:

Invite one of the children to be a volunteer. Tell everyone that there are some coins hidden around the room. Invite others to watch as the volunteer searches for all of the hidden coins.

After the volunteer has found all of the coins, place them on a table or in another place where everyone can see them.

Explain: When we are baptized, we receive the gift of the Holy Ghost. And through the Holy Ghost, each of us can receive some spiritual powers called Gifts of the Spirit. Heavenly Father gives spiritual gifts to each of us! Heavenly Father has told us to seek these gifts, just like the volunteer had to seek and look for these coins!

▶ VIDEO:

Say: "We are going to watch a video about gifts of the spirit! See if you can find the gifts, and see if you can remember what some of the gifts are."

[Watch Video: "Gifts of the Spirit | Animated Scripture Lesson for Kids"]

Discuss the following questions after watching the video:

1) What are some of the gifts of the spirit? (*Faith, Believing that Jesus is the Christ, Healing, Knowledge, Miracles, Languages, Teaching by the power of the Holy Ghost.*)

2) Does everyone receive a gift of the Spirit from Heavenly Father? (*Yes.*)

3) Does everyone receive all the gifts? (*No, everyone receives different gifts.*)

📖 SCRIPTURE:

Read the verses below and discuss the questions that follow.

[D&C 46:8]

"...seek ye earnestly the best gifts, always remembering for what they are given;"

1) What does it mean to seek something "earnestly?" (*It means really trying to find it.*)

[D&C 46:11]

11 For all have not every gift given unto them; for there are many gifts, and to every man is given a gift by the Spirit of God.

1) How many gifts of the spirit are there? (*There are many gifts.*)

2) How many people receive a gift of the spirit? (*Everyone!*)

3) How are the gifts given to us? (*By the spirit of God.*)

[D&C 46:12]

12 To some is given one, and to some is given another, that all may be profited thereby.

1) Why does Heavenly Father give us spiritual gifts? (*So that all may profit from them.*)

✏️ ACTIVITY PAGES:

[Pass out activity pages]

Invite children to color complete the activity page! Color the tokens that represent the gifts of the spirit, then color the presents on the other page. Cut on the dotted lines to make paper "doors" that can open and close. Glue or tape the presents paper on top of the "tokens" paper so that the open doors reveal the gifts of the spirit. Invite the children to "seek" the gifts of the spirit by opening the doors. Use this time to talk about the gifts of the spirit that are given through the Holy Ghost.

 TESTIMONY:

Bear testimony of the truths found in the scriptures.

This page intentionally left blank.

Gifts of the Spirit

"...seek ye earnestly the best gifts, always remembering for what they are given..."

-D&C 46:8

This page intentionally left blank.

Directions:

1) Color the badges below! These badges represent some of the gifts of the spirit.
2) Color the presents on the other page.
3) Cut on all of the dotted lines and then fold on the solito make a paper "door" that can be opened and closed.
4) Glue or tape the "presents" page over the top of the "badges" page. Open the doors to reveal the gifts of the spirit!

Faith

Testimony

Knowledge

Healing

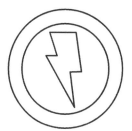

Miracles

Teaching with the Holy Ghost

Languages

This page intentionally left blank.

Week 21: May 19 - 25

 D&C 49-50

 TOPIC | That Which is of God is Light

♪ **OPENING SONG** "Search, Ponder, and Pray"

✐ PREPARATION:

You will need a backpack, and you will need 5-10 potatoes (or other objects of similar size such as apples, oranges, rocks, or tennis balls).

🗩 INTRODUCTION:

Invite a volunteer to stand in the front of the room. Tell the volunteer to try to hold all of the potatoes in only one hand. Start handing the potatoes to the volunteer one at a time and see how many they can hold before they begin to drop the potatoes!

Next, give the backpack to the volunteer and repeat the activity. Tell the volunteer they can use this backpack to "receive" the potatoes and hold them securely! Give the potatoes to the volunteer one at a time again, making sure they have enough time to "receive" the potatoes and load them into the backpack.

When you have finished the activity, discuss the following questions:

1) How many potatoes could the volunteer hold in one hand? *(Discuss.)*

2) Was the volunteer able to "receive" all of the potatoes that they were given? *(No.)*

3) How many potatoes could the volunteer hold with the backpack? *(All of them!)*

4) Was the volunteer able to "receive" all of the potatoes this time? *(Yes!)*

Explain: When Heavenly Father teaches us truth, we have a choice to make. We can open our heart and receive it (like the backpack), or we can close our heart and choose not to receive it. If our heart is open, then Heavenly Father can keep giving us more and more truth!

▶ VIDEO:

Say: Now we are going to watch a video about fireflies! In the scriptures, light is a symbol for truth. Let's watch and see what the fireflies teach us about receiving spiritual truth from Heavenly Father!

[Watch Video: "Merrick and the Fireflies | Animated Scripture Lesson for Kids"]

Discuss the following questions after watching the video:

1) What did the fireflies teach Merrick about receiving spiritual light from Heavenly Father? *(Heavenly Father gives us spiritual light a little at a time.)*

2) The lights are a symbol for something. Do you remember what the lights represent? *(Heavenly Father, truth, spiritual light.)*

3) What should we do when Heavenly Father gives us a little bit of spiritual light? *(We need to open our heart and receive it!)*

4) If we receive the light that He gives us, what will happen next? *(He will give us more light!)*

📖 SCRIPTURE:

Read the verses below and discuss the questions that follow.

[D&C 50:24]

24 *"That which is of God is light; and he that receiveth light, and continueth in God, receiveth more light..."*

1) What is light a symbol for?" *(That which is "of God.")*

2) If we receive things of God and continue in God, what will happen next? *(We will be given more light!)*

3) How can we open our hearts and "receive" that light that God gives us? *(Discuss.)*

[John 8:12]

12 *"Then spake Jesus again unto them, saying, I am the light of the world: he that followeth me shall not walk in darkness, but shall have the light of life."*

    1) What is the light a symbol of in this verse? *(Jesus Christ.)*

    2) How can we open our hearts and "receive" the light of Jesus Christ? *(Discuss!)*

[2 Nephi 28:30]

30 For behold, thus saith the Lord God: I will give unto the children of men line upon line, precept upon precept, here a little and there a little; and blessed are those who hearken unto my precepts, and lend an ear unto my counsel, for they shall learn wisdom; for unto him that receiveth I will give more..."

    1) How does Heavenly Father give truth to us? *(Line upon line, here a little, there a little.)*

    2) If we receive the things Heavenly Father teaches us, what will happen next? *(He will give more!)*

♡ TESTIMONY:

[Pass out activity pages]

Invite children to color the scene from the video. Read the scripture on the coloring page together. Use this time to discuss spiritual light, and receiving truth a little at a time.

ACTIVITY PAGES:

Bear testimony of the truths found in the scriptures.

This page intentionally left blank.

"That which is of God is light; and he that receiveth light, and continueth in God, receiveth more light..."

-D&C 50:24

This page intentionally left blank.

Week 22: May 26 - Jun 1

 D&C 51-57

 TOPIC | Honesty

OPENING SONG "Choose the Right"

PREPARATION:

You will need some yarn or string. Before the lesson, use a lot of the yarn to make a tangled up mess with many knots in it that would be difficult to untangle. Use another (smaller) piece of yarn to tie a single knot, very loosely, that could easily be loosened and untied.

💬 INTRODUCTION ACTIVITY:

Set a time limit and invite the children to take turns trying to straighten out the tangled mess! The tangles should be bad enough that it's impossible to untangle quickly.

Next, ask for a volunteer to untangle the string with a single (loose) knot.

When you have finished the activity, discuss the following questions:

1) Was it easy to untangle these knots? (Discuss.)

2) Which one was easier? Why? (Discuss.)

3) Which one was more difficult? Why? (Discuss.)

Explain: God has taught us that it is very important to be honest. Being honest means to tell the truth. When we are honest with ourselves, honest with others, and honest with Heavenly Father, we can feel peace in our hearts and we can feel the Holy Ghost. (Hold up the untangled string.)

But if we choose to be dishonest, we won't feel peace in our hearts and we won't be able to feel the Holy Ghost. (Hold up the tangled ball of string.) Our hearts can feel like a tangled mess!

▶ VIDEO:

Say: Now we are going to watch a video about a robot whose wires get tangled up when he chooses to tell a lie. Let's watch and see what happens when the wires get tangled up!

[Watch Video: "Tangled Wires | A Story About Honesty"]

Discuss the following questions after watching the video:

1) What happened when the robot decided to tell a lie? (*His wires got tangled up and everything stopped working!*)

2) What did the robot have to do to untangle the wires? (*He needed to tell the truth.*)

3) If it's bad for the robot, why did the robot choose to be dishonest? (*He wanted the speaker box!*)

4) How can the robot remember to be honest next time, even if he wants something? (*Discuss.*)

5) Why do our hearts feel like tangled up wires when we are dishonest? (*Because we don't feel peace, and we can't feel the Holy Ghost as much.*)

📖 SCRIPTURE:

Read the verses below and discuss the questions that follow.

[D&C 51:9]

9 And let every man deal honestly, and be alike among this people, and receive alike, that ye may be one, even as I have commanded you.

1) Were the robots in the video dealing honestly with each other?" (*Not at first, but then they did in the end.*)

2) What do you think it means to "deal honestly" with each other? (*Discuss.*)

[D&C 3:2]

2 For God doth not walk in crooked paths, neither doth he turn to the right hand nor to the left, neither doth he vary from that which he hath said, therefore his paths are straight, and his course is one eternal round.

    1) Do you think Heavenly Father has a tangled up heart? *(No! He does not walk in crooked paths and His paths are straight! He does not lie!)*

[Exodus 20:16]

16 Thou shalt not bear false witness against thy neighbour.

    1) What does it mean to "bear false witness?" *(It means to tell a lie.)*

    2) Who is speaking in this verse? *(God is speaking to Moses. He is giving him the Ten Commandments.)*

ACTIVITY PAGES:

[Pass out activity pages]

Invite the children to draw straight wires that are working inside the robot who is being honest. Next, invite the children to draw a messy knot of tangled wires that aren't working inside the robot who is being dishonest!

♡ TESTIMONY:

Bear testimony of the truths found in the scriptures.

This page intentionally left blank.

Draw some straight wires that are working well to show the peace we feel in our hearts when we are honest!

This page intentionally left blank.

Draw some tangled up wires that are not working well to show how we feel in hour hearts when we are dishonet!

www.LatterDayKids.com

This page intentionally left blank.

Week 23: June 2 - 8

 D&C 58-59

 TOPIC | Anxiously Engaged in a Good Cause

 OPENING SONG "When We're Helping We're Happy"

✍ PREPARATION:

Print a copy of the "Imagination Circle Challenge" for each person who will be present at the lesson. Also have pencils, markers, or crayons ready for everyone to use.

💬 INTRODUCTION ACTIVITY:

Pass out a copy of the "Imagination Circle Challenge" to each person. Invite the children to use their imagination to think of something that the circle could be, and then draw it! (For example, if a child thought of a sun they would draw sun rays around the circle to show that it is a sun.) Try to encourage each child to generate an idea on their own! If a child is having a difficult time with this, you could invite them to walk around the house on their own and look for things that are circles.

Once everyone has finished their drawings, have the children take turns sharing the drawings with the rest of the group and telling the group what they imagined!

Once you have completed the activity, discuss the following questions.

1) Did someone tell you what to draw? Or did you think of it all by yourself? (*They thought of the ideas by themselves!*)

2) Do you know what the word "imagination" means? (*It means to think of an idea in your mind.*)

151

3) Why do you think Heavenly Father wanted us to have an imagination? *(Discuss.)*

4) Do you think Heavenly Father wants us to use our imagination for good things or bad things? *(Good things.)*

V I D E O :

Say: Now we are going to watch a video about some roly polies! Let's watch and see if the roly polies use their imagination to do good things!

[Watch Video: "Joey the Roly Poly | Animated Scripture Lesson for Kids"]

Discuss the following questions after watching the video:

1) Why were the roly polies waiting by the box? *(They were waiting for the box to tell them what to do.)*

2) Did the box help them do good things? *(Yes!)*

3) What happened when the roly polies used their imagination? *(They were able to do even more good things!)*

4) What were some of the ideas that the roly polies had? How many can you remember? *(Discuss.)*

5) How are we like the roly polies? *(We have an imagination! And Heavenly Father has given us the power to think of lots of good things to do!)*

SCRIPTURE:

Read the first part of D&C 58:27 and discuss the questions that follow.

[D&C 58:27]

27 Verily I say, men should be anxiously engaged in a good cause,

1) What does it mean to be "anxiously engaged?" *(It means you really want to do something and you are trying hard to do it.)*

2) What is a "good cause?" *(It means something that is good.)*

Read D&C 58:27 again, but this time read the entire verse. Then discuss the questions that follow.

[D&C 58:27]

27 Verily I say, men should be anxiously engaged in a good cause, and do many things of their own free will, and bring to pass much righteousness;

    1) What does it mean to do something of our "own free will?" *(It means we are doing it because we want to, and not because someone is making us do it.)*

    2) What does it mean to "bring to pass much righteousness?" *(It means using your imagination and working hard to make good things happen!)*

[D&C 58:27]

28 For the power is in them, wherein they are agents unto themselves. And inasmuch as men do good they shall in nowise lose their reward.

    1) Who has "power in them" to do good things? *(We all do!)*

    2) What do you think that power is? *(Imagination, creativity, hard work, faith.)*

    3) What does Heavenly Father want us to use that power for? *(To do good things!)*

ACTIVITY PAGES:

[Pass out activity pages]

Invite the children to color the scene from the video! As they are coloring, ask the children how many good things they can think of to do with their imagination. Invite them to write or draw their ideas on the back of the paper. You could also print extra copies of the "Imagination Circle Challenge" and invite them to think of more ideas for what the circle could be!

♡ TESTIMONY:

Bear testimony of the truths found in the scriptures.

This page intentionally left blank.

Imagination Circle Challenge

What do you think this could this circle could be? Use your imagination, and then draw what you imagined!

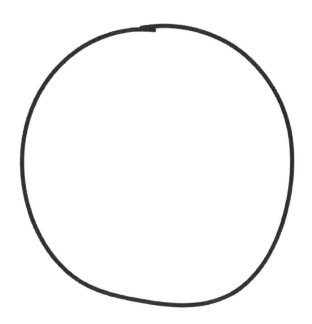

This page intentionally left blank.

"Verily I say, men should be aanxiously engaged in a good cause, and do many things of their own free will, and bring to pass much righteousness..."

-D&C 58:27

This page intentionally left blank.

Week 24: Jun 9 - 15

 D&C 60-63

 TOPIC | Divine Attributes of Jesus Christ

 OPENING SONG "I Stand All Amazed"

 PREPARATION:

You will need a rock, some water, some bread, and a small light.

🗩 INTRODUCTION ACTIVITY:

Place the objects on the table and ask the children to describe each item, one at a time. Try to encourage discussion about each item, what it does, how it can help us, etc. For example: A rock is firm, hard, immovable, sturdy, a good foundation, etc. Water gives life, we can't live without it, water cleans and washes us, etc.

When you have finished talking about each item, discuss the following questions:

1) The scriptures teach us that Jesus Christ is the rock on which we should build. How do you think Jesus Christ is like a rock? *(Discuss.)*

2) The scriptures teach us that Jesus Christ is the living water. How do you think Jesus Christ is like water? *(Discuss.)*

3) The scriptures teach us that Jesus Christ is the bread of life. How do you think Jesus Christ is like bread? *(Discuss.)*

4) The scriptures teach us that Jesus Christ is the light of the world. How do you think Jesus Christ is like a light? *(Discuss.)*

▶ VIDEO:

Say: Now we are going to watch a video about more attributes of Jesus Christ. See if you can remember four things from this video that the scriptures teach us about Jesus Christ.

[Watch Video: "Divine Attributes of Jesus Christ | Animated Scripture Lesson for Kids"]

Discuss the following questions after watching the video:

1) Can you remember the four attributes of Jesus Christ that were shown in the video? (*He is powerful, he knows all things, he keeps his promises, and he loves all of us!*)

2) Why do we need to learn about Jesus Christ? (*Knowing about him can help us have stronger faith in Him!*)

3) Where can we learn about Jesus Christ? (*In the scriptures.*)

4) Can you think of any other things that you have learned about Jesus Christ from the scriptures? (*Discuss.*)

📖 SCRIPTURE:

Read the verses below and discuss the questions that follow.

[D&C 61:1]

1 Behold, and hearken unto the voice of him who has all power, who is from everlasting to everlasting, even Alpha and Omega, the beginning and the end.

1) What can we learn about Jesus Christ from this scripture?" (*He has all power.*)

[John 15:9]

9 As the Father hath loved me, so have I loved you: continue ye in my love.

1) What can we learn about Jesus Christ from this scripture?" (*He loves us.*)

[1 Nephi 9:6]

6 But the Lord knoweth all things from the beginning; wherefore, he prepareth a way to accomplish all his works among the children of men; for behold, he hath all power unto the fulfilling of all his words.

> 1) What can we learn about Jesus Christ from this scripture?" (*He knows all things, he has all power, and he will fulfill all his words and keep his promises.*)

ACTIVITY PAGES:

[Pass out activity pages]

Invite the children to color the "Divine Attributes of Jesus Christ" activity page. Use this time to talk about Jesus Christ and why we can have strong faith in Him.

♡ TESTIMONY:

Bear testimony of the truths found in the scriptures.

This page intentionally left blank.

Divine Attributes of Jesus Christ

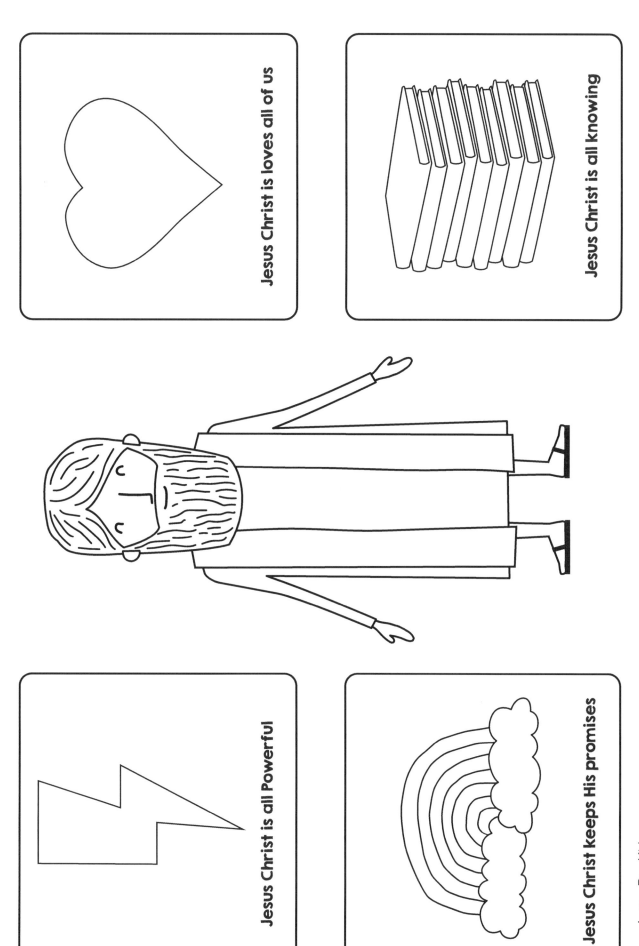

Jesus Christ is loves all of us

Jesus Christ is all knowing

Jesus Christ is all Powerful

Jesus Christ keeps His promises

www.LatterDayKids.com

This page intentionally left blank.

Week 25: Jun 16 - 22

 D&C 64-66

 TOPIC | The Lord Requireth the Heart and a Willing Mind

 OPENING SONG "Keep the Commandments"

 PREPARATION:

You will need a towel or small blanket for each child!

💬 INTRODUCTION ACTIVITY:

Give a towel to each person who is present, and give everyone a space on the floor where they can lay the towel flat. Explain that you are going to give them a challenge, but the real contest is to see who can be the most whiny while they complete the challenge! Encourage everyone to be whiny with their voices, whiny with their faces, and whiny with their arms and body language!

Tell them that the challenge is to fold the towel. Remind everyone to be as whiny as possible and to complain, moan, murmur, etc. while they are folding the towels).

Once you have completed the activity, collect the towels and discuss the following questions.

1) Was it easy to fold the towel when you were being whiny? (*Hopefully they obeyed quickly!*)

2) How did the towels turn out? Were they folded neatly? (*Discuss.*)

3) How did it feel to be whiny? If we chose to whine all the time, do you think things would be easier or more difficult? (*Discuss.*)

4) Do you think Jesus Christ ever whines or complains when Heavenly Father asks Him to do something? (*No.*)

5) What does Jesus do instead? *(He obeys Heavenly Father.)*

6) What do you think is the opposite of whining? *(Obedience with a good attitude.)*

Explain: Today we are going to learn about obedience. When we choose to obey Heavenly Father, we must try with all our hearts, and we must be willing to do what Heavenly Father asks us to do.

▶ VIDEO:

Now we are going to watch a video about a whiny whale! Let's watch and see what whale was whining about!

[Watch Video: "The Whiny Whale | Animated Scripture Lesson for Kids"]

Discuss the following questions after watching the video:

1) What was the whiny whale whining about? *(He didn't want to swim to the big rock.)*

2) What did the other whales do? *(They tried with all their hearts, and they were willing to do what the coach asked them to do.)*

3) Why did the whiny whale choose to follow the coach? *(Because he wanted to swim faster.)*

4) If the whiny whale only whines, will he be able to swim faster? *(No.)*

5) How is the coach like Jesus Christ? *(Jesus Christ wants to teach us how to be like Him, and help us return to Heavenly Father.)*

6) If we want to be like Jesus Christ, what do we have to do? *(We have to try with all our hearts, and we must be willing to do what Jesus Christ asks us to do.)*

📖 SCRIPTURE:

Read the following scriptures and discuss the questions that follow.

[Read D&C 64:34]

34 Behold, the Lord requireth the heart and a willing mind; and the willing and obedient shall eat the good of the land of Zion in these last days.

1) Why does the Lord require our heart? *(Discuss.)*

2) What do you think it means to give the Lord our heart? *(Discuss.)*

3) Why does the Lord require a willing mind? *(Discuss.)*

4) What do you think it means to have a willing mind? *(Discuss.)*

[Read Abraham 3:25]

25 And we will prove them herewith, to see if they will do all things whatsoever the Lord their God shall command them;

1) Who is speaking in this verse? *(Heavenly Father.)*

2) What does it mean to "prove" someone? *(To test them.)*

3) What is Heavenly Father testing us on? *(To see if we are willing to do all that God commands us.)*

 ## ACTIVITY PAGES:

Invite Children to color the "Whiny Whale" coloring page. Invite the children to think of something that Heavenly Father has asked them to do and to think about how they can try with all their heart and be willing to do it.

 ## TESTIMONY:

Bear testimony of the truths found in the scriptures.

This page intentionally left blank.

"The Lord requireth the heart and a willing mind."

-D&C 64:34

This page intentionally left blank.

Week 26: June 23 - 29

 D&C 67-70

 TOPIC | Baptism

 **OPENING SONG** "Baptism"

PREPARATION:

You will need a piece of green paper, a piece of red paper, two popsicle sticks and tape! Cut a tennis ball-sized circle from each sheet of paper and attach each circle to a popsicle stick. You are making signs that you can hold up to represent a green light and a red light. If you do not have popsicle sticks, you can also use pencils.

INTRODUCTION ACTIVITY:

Play "Red Light, Green Light!" Invite the children to stand on one side of the room while a volunteer stands on the other side of the room with the two "traffic lights." When the volunteer holds up the green light, participants may begin walking, but when the volunteer holds up the red light, they must stop. The goal is to reach the traffic lights! The first person to make it to the traffic lights gets to hold up the traffic lights for the next round!

Play until all the children have had a turn to hold the "traffic lights."

Once you have completed the activity, discuss the following questions.

1) How did you know when to go? (*The green light was showing!*)

2) How did you know when to stop? (*The red light was showing!*)

3) How did you know what the colors mean? (*Discuss.*)

Explain: The green and red lights are symbols. Symbols can help us learn things and they can help us remember things. When Heavenly Father teaches us, He often uses symbols! Today we are going to learn about the symbols of baptism.

▶ VIDEO:

Now we are going to watch a video about the symbols of baptism! See if you can remember what the symbols mean!

[Watch Video: "Symbols of Baptism | Animated Scripture Lesson for Kids"]

Discuss the following questions after watching the video:

1) Why do we wear white clothes when we are baptized? What does that symbol mean? (It represents being pure like Jesus Christ.)

2) Why do we get baptized in water? What does that symbol mean? (Because water is used to wash things, and it's a symbol for being clean.)

3) Why do we go down under the water? What does that symbol mean? (It's a symbol for when Jesus Christ was buried, and it also is a symbol for burying our old sins.)

4) When we come back out of the water, what does that remind us of? What does that symbol mean? (It's a symbol of Christ's resurrection, and it also is a symbol for being born again with a new heart.)

5) When we take the sacrament, what does the bread represent? What does that symbol mean? (It's a symbol for the body of Jesus Christ.)

6) When we take the sacrament, what does the water represent? What does that symbol mean? (It's a symbol for the blood of Jesus Christ.)

📖 SCRIPTURE:

Read the following scriptures and discuss the questions that follow.

[Read D&C 68:27]

27 And their children shall be baptized for the remission of their sins when eight years old, and receive the laying on of the hands.

1) Who was the Lord talking to in this verse? (*To members of the church who had children!*)

2) What did the Lord tell the parents to do? (*To teach their children about baptism and to baptize them when they are eight years old.*)

[Read John 3:3-5]

3 Jesus answered and said unto him, Verily, verily, I say unto thee, Except a man be born again, he cannot see the kingdom of God.

4 Nicodemus saith unto him, How can a man be born when he is old? can he enter the second time into his mother's womb, and be born?

5 Jesus answered, Verily, verily, I say unto thee, Except a man be born of water and of the Spirit, he cannot enter into the kingdom of God.

1) What was Jesus talking about when He said we must be born again? (*He was teaching about baptism.*)

2) When we are baptized, what is the symbol for being born again? (*Coming back up out of the water is a symbol for being born again.*)

[Read Matthew 3:16]

16 And Jesus, when he was baptized, went up straightway out of the water: and, lo, the heavens were opened unto him, and he saw the Spirit of God descending like a dove, and lighting upon him:

1) Who was baptized in this verse? (*Jesus Christ was baptized.*)

2) What was Jesus coming up out of the water, what was that a symbol for? (*It's a symbol for being born again and for Jesus Christ's resurrection.*)

ACTIVITY PAGES:

[Pass out coloring page]

Invite children to complete the "symbols" matching activity. Use this time to talk about the symbols of baptism and the meaning behind the symbols.

♡ TESTIMONY:

Bear testimony of the truths found in the scriptures.

This page intentionally left blank.

"Symbols of Baptism" Matching Game

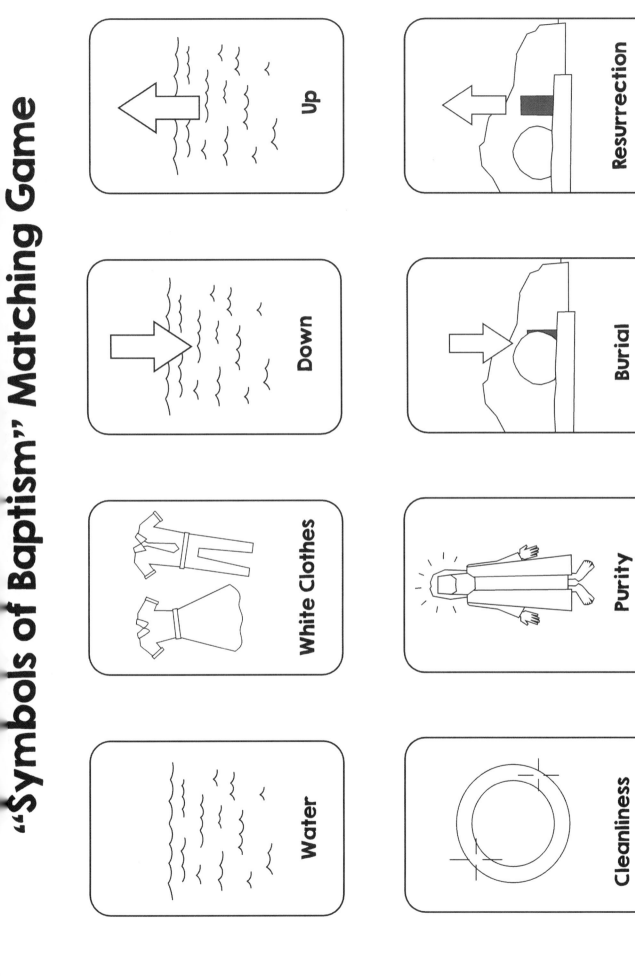

Up

Resurrection

Down

Burial

White Clothes

Purity

Water

Cleanliness

This page intentionally left blank.

Week 27: Jun 30 – Jul 6

 D&C 71-75

 TOPIC | Labor With Your Might

🎵 **OPENING SONG** "I Will Follow God's Plan"

✒ PREPARATION:

You will need a handful of dry beans (any type) and a small jar. You will also need empty wall space (that several people could lean against).

💬 INTRODUCTION ACTIVITY:

Invite everyone to do the "wall sit" exercise! You'll use the beans to count how long everyone can hold the pose by placing one bean at a time into the jar. Tell them that the goal is to get as many beans in the jar as they can! Keep adding beans to the jar until the last person quits the challenge.

Once you have completed the activity, invite everyone to return to their seats. Count the beans and allow everyone to catch their breath! Explain that you did this activity to help everyone understand what hard work feels like.

1) Was this challenge harder at the beginning? Or at the end? (*At the end!*)

2) So when were you doing the most work? (*At the end.*)

3) In this activity, you were working hard to stay sitting against the wall! What other things can you think of that you could work hard for? (*Discuss ideas!*)

4) Is work a bad thing? Or is work a good thing? (*A good thing.*)

5) Why is work a good thing? (*Discuss good things that come from work such as: growth, learning, health, strength, skills, confidence, etc.*)

6) Do you think Heavenly Father and Jesus Christ know how to work hard? *(Yes.)*

7) Do you think Heavenly Father wants us to learn how to work hard? Why? *(Discuss.)*

▶ VIDEO:

Now we are going to watch a video about a baby elephant named Bastian! Bastian has a goal that he really wants to accomplish. Let's see if Bastian knows how to work hard to accomplish his goal!

[Watch Video: "Bastian the Baby Elephant | A Story about Hard Work"]

Discuss the following questions after watching the video:

1) What was Bastian's goal? *(He wanted to participate in "The Great Rock Pull!")*

2) What did Bastian have to do to accomplish his goal? *(He had to work hard!)*

3) Why didn't Bastian stop at the finish line? Why did he keep going? *(He wanted to do his very best!)*

4) How do you think Bastian felt after he worked hard and did his very best? *(Very happy!)*

5) Do you think Heavenly Father wants all of us to feel like that? *(Yes.)*

📖 SCRIPTURE:

Read the following scriptures and discuss the questions that follow.

[Read Moses 1:39]

39 For behold, this is my work and my glory—to bring to pass the immortality and eternal life of man.

1) Does Heavenly Father have work to do? *(Yes!)*

2) What is Heavenly Father's work? *(To bring to pass the immortality and eternal life of man.)*

[Read D&C 75:3]

3 Behold, I say unto you that it is my will that you should go forth and not tarry, neither be idle but labor with your might—

1) What does it mean to be "idle?" *(Being idle means to avoid work, or be lazy.)*

2) Instead of being idle, what does the Lord want us to do? *(Labor with our might!)*

3) What does "labor with our might" mean? *(It means to work as hard as we can!)*

[Read John 5:17]

17 But Jesus answered them, My Father worketh hitherto, and I work.

1) Who is speaking in this verse? *(Jesus.)*

2) What did He say? *(He works, and Heavenly Father works.)*

 ## ACTIVITY PAGES:

[Pass out coloring page]

Invite Children to color the "Labor With Your Might" coloring page. Use this time to discuss the principle of work, and how it can bless our lives.

 ## TESTIMONY:

Bear testimony of the truths found in the scriptures.

This page intentionally left blank.

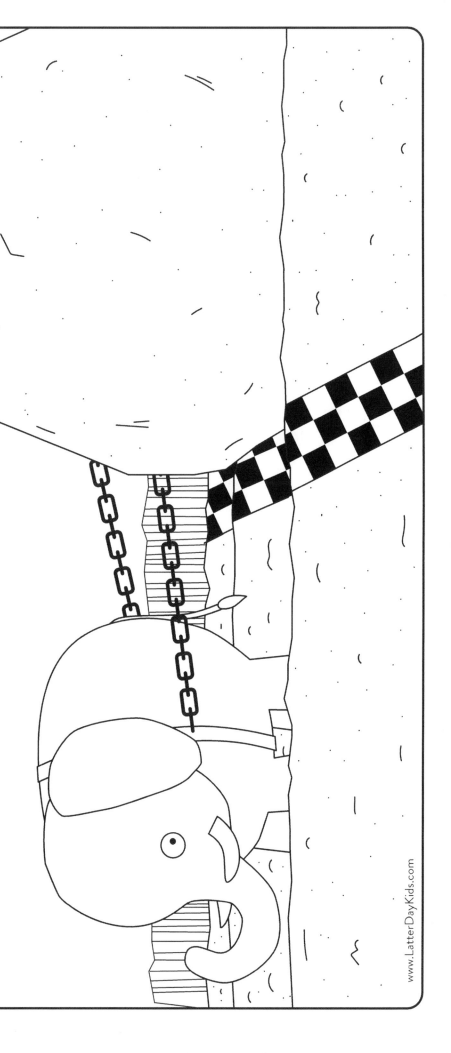

"...labor with your might."

-D&C 75:3

www.LatterDayKids.com

This page intentionally left blank.

Week 28: Jul 7 - 13

 D&C 76

 TOPIC | We Are All Children of God

🎵 **OPENING SONG** "I am a Child of God"

✍️ **PREPARATION:**

Gather some seeds! Packets of seeds (with photos on the outside), and more than one type of seed would be ideal. But something as simple as some popcorn kernels will work.

(*If you don't have access to seeds or popcorn kernels, you can find pictures of different types of seeds and their parent plants on the internet, to show your family.)*

💬 **INTRODUCTION ACTIVITY:**

Lay out the seeds on a table or on the floor, and label each type. Invite everyone to examine the **different types of seeds.** (*Or show pictures of seeds and their parent plants that you found on the internet.)*

As the children look at the seeds, discuss the following questions.

1) What are these? *(Seeds!)*

2) Where do the seeds come from? *(From the original plant! Explain that corn seeds come from corn, pumpkin seeds come from pumpkins, etc.)*

3) If you plant these seeds in some soil and take care of them, what will happen? *(They will each grow and become the same plant that they each came from!)*

4) If we are children of Heavenly Father, what do you think that means? (*It means we can become like our heavenly parents!*)

5) How are we like the seeds? (*Discuss.*)

6) How is Heavenly Father like the full grown plants? (*Discuss.*)

▶ VIDEO:

Now we are going to watch a video about some baby animals. The baby animals want to be like their parents when they grow up. Do you think they can be like their parents?

[Watch Video: "We Are All Children of God | Animated Scripture Lesson for Kids"]

Discuss the following questions after watching the video:

1) What did the baby lion see when he watched his father? (*He saw that his father was big and strong and had a loud roar!*)

2) Could the baby lion do all the things that his father could do? (*Not yet.*)

3) What will happen after a long time? (*The baby lion will be like his father, and he will be able to do all the things his father can do!*)

4) What did the baby bird see when she watched her mother? (*She saw that her mother could fly high in the sky!*)

5) Could the baby bird do all the things that her mother could do? (*Not yet.*)

6) What will happen after a long time? (*The baby bird will be just like her mother, and she will be able to do all the things her mother can do!*)

7) How are we like the baby animals? (*We are learning to be like Heavenly Father, just like the baby animals were learning to be like their parents.*)

📖 SCRIPTURE:

Read the following scriptures and discuss the questions that follow.

[D&C 76:24]

24 That by him, and through him, and of him, the worlds are and were created, and the inhabitants thereof are begotten sons and daughters unto God.

    1) What are inhabitants? *(All the people who live on the earth.)*

    2) Who are God's sons and daughters? *(All of us!)*

[Acts 17:29]

29 Forasmuch then as we are the offspring of God, we ought not to think that the Godhead is like unto gold, or silver, or stone, graven by art and man's device.

    1) **What does offspring mean?** *(It's another way to say children.)*

    2) Did we make God? Or did God make us? *(God made us, we did not make God.)*

[Genesis 1:26]

26 And God said, Let us make man in our image, after our likeness...

    1) Who did God make us to be like? *(He made us to be like Him!)*

    2) Can we do everything God can do right now? *(No.)*

    3) Why not? *(Because we are still little, like the baby lion and the baby bird.)*

 ## ACTIVITY PAGES:

[Pass out coloring page]

Invite Children to color the "We are all Children of God" coloring page. Use this time to discuss the doctrine that we are sons and daughters of God.

 ## TESTIMONY:

Bear testimony of the truths found in the scriptures.

This page intentionally left blank.

We are all children of God!

This page intentionally left blank.

Week 29: July 14-20

 D&C 77-80

 TOPIC | I Will Lead You Along

 **OPENING SONG** "Come Follow Me"

✏ PREPARATION:

Hide a series of clues that ultimately leads to an image of Jesus Christ. Each clue should lead to the next clue. The clues should be simple, such as "look in the pantry," or "look under the bathroom sink."

💬 INTRODUCTION ACTIVITY:

Give the first clue to the children and invite them to follow the clues until they find the image of Jesus Christ.

After the children have found all the clues and the image of Christ, ask the following questions:

1) When you began this activity, did you know where it was going to end? *(No.)*

2) How did you get to the end? *(By following each clue, one at a time.)*

3) If you were in a hurry and you tried to skip one of the clues, what would have happened? *(It would have taken even longer to get to the end!)*

4) What was the best way to find the image of Jesus Christ? *(To follow the clues step by step.)*

Explain: Heavenly Father is leading us to Him, just like this activity. If we follow Him one step at a time, He will show us the way. But, we have to trust Him and keep following the steps! Now we are going to watch a video about a father who has a surprise for his kids! But, the kids have to follow their father's directions, step by step. Let's watch and see if they will follow his directions!

▶ VIDEO:

[Watch Video: "I Will Lead You Along | A Story About Following Jesus Christ"]

Discuss the following questions after watching the video:

1) Did the children follow all of their father's directions and find the treasure? *(Yes!)*

2) Why were the children complaining at first? *(Because they thought that their father was going the wrong way.)*

3) What would have happened if the children ignored their father and went straight to Treasure Mountain? *(They wouldn't have been able to reach the cave without the ladder, the tunnel would have been too dark without the lamp, and they wouldn't have been able to open the treasure chest without the key!)*

4) How is Heavenly Father like the father in this story? *(He has wonderful things prepared for us, and He knows the way, and He knows everything that we will need along the way!)*

5) How are we like the children? *(We must learn to trust Heavenly Father and follow Him, one step at a time.)*

📖 SCRIPTURE:

Read the following scriptures and discuss the questions that follow.

[D&C 78:18]

18 And ye cannot bear all things now; nevertheless, be of good cheer, for I will lead you along. The kingdom is yours and the blessings thereof are yours, and the riches of eternity are yours.

1) Why doesn't Heavenly Father give us everything right now? *(We cannot bear all things right now. We're not ready.)*

2) What did He promise us? *(He will lead us along!)*

3) Can we still follow Him step by step, even if we don't know everything? *(Yes!)*

[2 Nephi 28:30]

30 For behold, thus saith the Lord God: I will give unto the children of men line upon line, precept upon precept, here a little and there a little...

1) Does God give us everything all at once? (No.)

2) How does He give things to us? (*He gives things to us line upon line, here a little and there a little.*)

[John 14:6]

6 Jesus saith unto him, I am the way, the truth, and the life: no man cometh unto the Father, but by me.

1) Who knows the way to Heavenly Father? (*Jesus Christ*)

2) Can you think of some things that Jesus Christ has taught us that we should do? (*Discuss.*)

3) What can we do to show Jesus Christ that we trust Him? (*Discuss.*)

✏ ACTIVITY PAGES:

[Pass out coloring page]

Invite Children to color the "I Will Lead You Along" coloring page. Use this time to discuss the importance of trusting the Lord and following Him one step at a time.

♡ TESTIMONY:

Bear testimony of the truths found in the scriptures.

This page intentionally left blank.

"For I will lead you along..."

-D&C 78:18

This page intentionally left blank.

Week 30: Jul 21 - 27

 D&C 81-83

 TOPIC | I Can Help People in Need

 **OPENING SONG** "Love One Another"

✐ PREPARATION:

You will need a hula hoop, or anything else that is flat, round, and large (like a pizza pan). You could also use a straight object, such as a yardstick.

💬 INTRODUCTION ACTIVITY:

You will be playing a variation of a group activity sometimes referred to as "Helium Hula Hoop." Invite all of the members of the group to stand in a circle and hold out their index fingers at waist level. Explain that their goal is to make sure that their fingers are always touching the hula hoop. Balance the hula hoop on everyone's fingers so that everyone's fingers are making contact, and then let go. (The hula hoop will rise into the air mysteriously!)

After you complete the activity, ask the following questions:

1) Was it hard to lift up the hula hoop? (*No, it was really easy!*)

2) All you were trying to do was touch the hula hoop, so why do you think the hula hoop went up in the air? (*Because every time someone touched the hula hoop, it went up a little more!*)

3) If everyone was trying not to touch the hula hoop, what do you think would happen? (*It would fall down to the ground!*)

Explain: Jesus Christ has asked us to love one another. He told us to succor the weak, to lift up the hands that hang down, and to strengthen the feeble knees. Did you know that lifting others is kind of like lifting the hula hoop! We just have to do our part.

1) What are some things that we can do to lift others? (*Discuss.*)

2) If everyone is willing to help others, what do you think will happen? (*Relate this to how easy it was to lift the hula hoop.*)

3) If no one is willing to help others, what do you think will happen? (*Discuss.*)

▶ VIDEO:

Now we are going to watch a video about a boy who doesn't want to help others. Later he changes his mind and decides to help others! Watch, and see if you can find out why he changes his mind!

[Watch Video: "The Bike Ride | A Story About Helping Others"]

Discuss the following questions after watching the video:

1) Why didn't the boy want to help others at first? (*He was not thinking about the other people and how they would feel. He was thinking about himself.*)

2) What happened that made him change his mind? (*The raccoon made fun of him and he felt sad, and then he understood how he was making the other animals feel.*)

3) What did he do? (*He found a way to help the other animals go fast with him on his bike so that they could have fun too!*)

4) Do you think Jesus Christ knows how other people are feeling? How do you think he knows? (*He suffered all things, and He understands how we feel.*)

📖 SCRIPTURE:

Read the following scriptures and discuss the questions that follow.

[D&C 81:5]

5 Wherefore, be faithful; stand in the office which I have appointed unto you; succor the weak, lift up the hands which hang down, and strengthen the feeble knees.

196

1) What does it mean to succor the weak? *(It means to help them.)*

2) When do our hands hang down? *(When we are sad or tired.)*

3) What are "feeble knees?" *(It means someone who is tired or weak.)*

4) What are some things we can do to help strengthen others? *(Discuss.)*

[John 13:34]

34 A new commandment I give unto you, That ye love one another; as I have loved you, that ye also love one another.

1) What did Jesus Christ command us to do? *(To love one another!)*

2) Who is our example for how to love one another? *(Jesus.)*

[John 13:35]

35 By this shall all men know that ye are my disciples, if ye have love one to another.

1) How will other people know that we follow Jesus Christ? *(They will know it when they see that we love one another.)*

2) What can we do to show that we love others, instead of just saying it? *(We can serve them and help them.)*

ACTIVITY PAGES:

[Pass out coloring page]

Invite Children to color the coloring page from the video. Use this time to discuss the importance of having compassion for others and finding ways to lift others up and help them.

♡ TESTIMONY:

Bear testimony of the truths found in the scriptures.

This page intentionally left blank.

"Succor the weak, lift up the hands which hang down, and strengthen the feeble knees."

-D&C 81:5

This page intentionally left blank.

LATTER DAY
KIDS

Week 31: Jul 28 - Aug 3

 D&C 84

 TOPIC | Priesthood Authority

 OPENING SONG "The Church of Jesus Christ"

☑ PREPARATION:

You will need your driver's license, and the "pretend" version of your driver's license provided on the last page of the lesson bundle. If you do not have access to a real driver's license, you could search the internet for an image of a driver's license.

💬 INTRODUCTION ACTIVITY:

Start by showing your real driver's license to the children. Pass it around so they can look at it. Discuss the following question as they are looking at the driver's license:

1) Do you know what this is? *(A driver's license!)*

2) What does it mean? *(It means you are allowed to drive on public roads!)*

3) If I show this to a police officer, would the officer let me drive? *(Yes!)*

Now, show your "pretend" driver's license to the children and discuss the following questions.

1) Here is a pretend driver's license. If I show this to a police officer, would the officer let me drive? *(No, we have to have the real one!)*

2) Why can't we make our own driver's licenses? *(We are not allowed to. We don't have the authority. We must go to someone who has the authority.)*

Hold up the two driver's licenses for comparison and explain the following: In order for a driver's license to work, it must be given by someone who has the authority. We have to follow their directions, and we must get permission from them to drive. If we don't have the authority and we try to do it by ourselves, it won't work, we would be breaking the law!

It's the same with priesthood ordinances. When we are baptized and when we take the sacrament, we can't just do those things by ourselves. Jesus Christ has the authority to lead His church, and we must follow His directions and we have to get permission from Him to do those things.

VIDEO:

Now we are going to watch a video about three animals who are racing in a go-kart race! But when the race ends, there is a problem. Watch and see if you can tell what the problem was.

[Watch Video: "The Go Kart Race | Animated Scripture Lesson for Kids"]

Discuss the following questions after watching the video:

1) What was the problem when the race ended? (*Lots of different people in the crowd tried to say who the winner was.*)

2) When the people in the crowd tried to say who the winner was, did it work? (*No.*)

3) Why not? (*Because they didn't have the authority.*)

4) Who had the authority to say who the winner was? (*Only the race director had the authority to say who the winner was.*)

5) Who has the authority to lead Jesus Christ's church? (*Jesus Christ.*)

6) If we want to do something in Jesus Christ's church, like baptisms, or the sacrament, can we do it by ourselves? (*No, it can only be done with Jesus Christ's authority.*)

SCRIPTURE:

Read the following scriptures and discuss the questions that follow.

[D&C 84:20]

20 Therefore, in the ordinances thereof, the power of godliness is manifest.

1) How is the power of godliness shown to us? (*Through priesthood ordinances.*)

2) What is a priesthood ordinance? (*An act or ceremony that is done by the authority of the priesthood.*)

[D&C 84:21]

21 And without the ordinances thereof, and the authority of the priesthood, the power of godliness is not manifest unto men in the flesh;

1) Can we perform priesthood ordinances if we don't have authority? (*No.*)

2) Who has the authority? (*Jesus Christ.*)

3) Does Jesus Christ give His authority to anyone else? (*Yes. It's called priesthood authority.*)

[Mark 1:22]

22 And they were astonished at his doctrine: for he taught them as one that had authority, and not as the scribes.

1) Who was teaching? (*Jesus Christ.*)

2) Why were they astonished when Jesus Christ was teaching them? (*Because he taught with authority.*)

[Mosiah 18:18]

18 And it came to pass that Alma, having authority from God, ordained priests; even one priest to every fifty of their number did he ordain to preach unto them, and to teach them concerning the things pertaining to the kingdom of God.

1) Who was ordaining priests? (*Alma.*)

2) Did Alma do it by himself? Or did he have the authority to do it? (*He had the authority.*)

3) Where did he get the authority? (*From God.*)

 ACTIVITY PAGES:

[Pass out coloring page]

Invite Children to color the coloring page from the video. Use this time to discuss the authority of Jesus Christ and priesthood authority.

♡ TESTIMONY:

Bear testimony of the truths found in the scriptures.

DRIVERS LICENSE

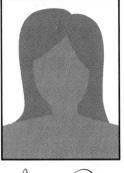

DL **123456789**   CLASS C

EXP **03/07/2034**

LN **DOE**

FN **JANE**
0123 ANYSTREET
ANYTOWN, CA 02045

DOB **03/07/1995**

DONOR

Jane Doe

| SEX F | HAIR BRN | EYES BLUE | ISS |
| HGT 5'6" | WGT 116 lb | | 03/07/2008 |

DRIVERS LICENSE

DL **123456789**   CLASS C

EXP **02/29/2034**

LN **DOE**

FN **JOHN**
0123 ANYSTREET
ANYTOWN, CA 02045

DOB **02/29/1992**

DONOR

John Doe

| SEX F | HAIR BRN | EYES BRN | ISS |
| HGT 6'2" | WGT 180 lb | | 02/29/2005 |

This page intentionally left blank.

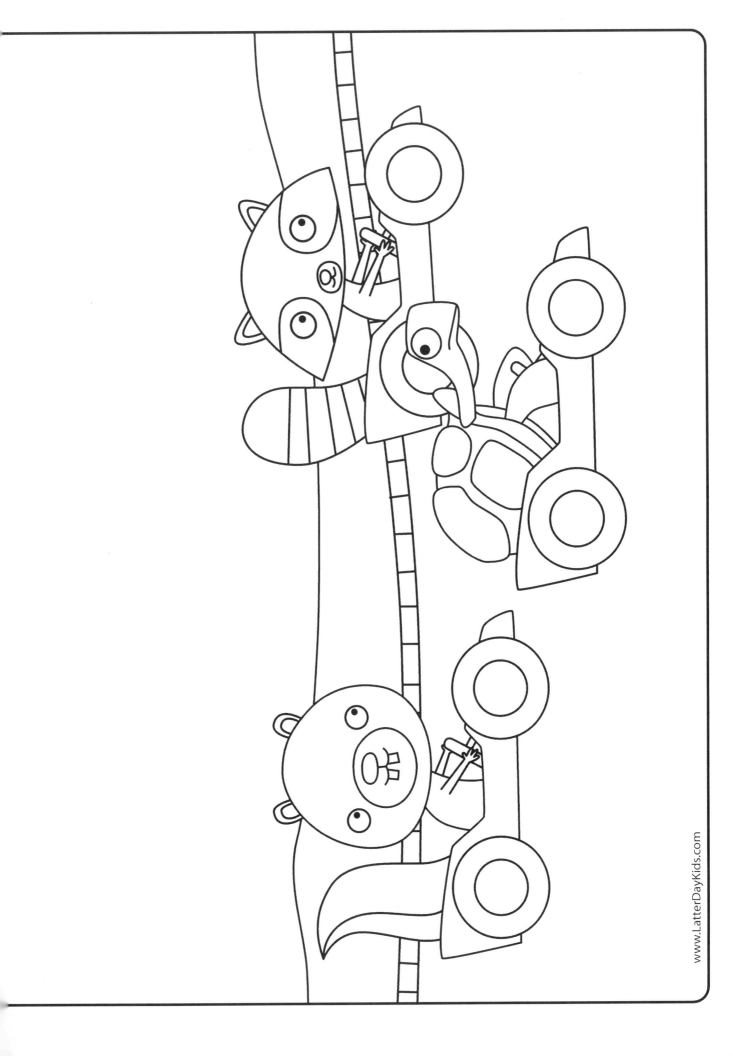

This page intentionally left blank.

LATTER DAY
KIDS

Week 32: Aug 4-10

 D&C 85-87

 TOPIC | The Still Small Voice

 OPENING SONG "The Holy Ghost"

🖋 PREPARATION:

Set a countdown timer on your phone for one minute, and choose a reverent sound for the ring tone. Turn the volume to a low setting.

💬 INTRODUCTION ACTIVITY:

Invite the children to leave the room while you hide your phone somewhere in the room. Start the 60 second timer and then invite the children to sit back down in their seats. Tell them that your phone will ring in 60 seconds, but it's very quiet! Tell them to listen carefully to see if they can hear the ring tone!

After you complete the activity, ask the following questions:

1) When you were trying to hear the phone, were you moving? Or were you sitting still? (Discuss.)

2) When you were trying to hear the phone, were you making noise, or were you silent? (Discuss.)

3) When you were trying to hear the phone, were you distracted? Or were you paying attention? (Discuss.)

4) What happened when you did all of those things? Were you able to hear the phone? (Yes!

Explain that in the scriptures, the Holy Ghost is sometimes called "The Still Small Voice." The still small voice is not loud. It's more like a whisper that we feel in our hearts, and if we want to hear it, we need to be still, and focus, and listen with our hearts - just like when we were listening to hear the phone!

▶ VIDEO:

Now we are going to watch a video about Olivia the Owl! Let's watch and see what Olivia learns about the still small voice!

[Watch Video: "Olivia the Owl | Animate Scripture Lesson for Kids"]

Discuss the following questions after watching the video:

1) Does the still small voice speak to us like a tornado? (No, it speaks to us like a gentle breeze.)

2) Does the still small voice speak to us like thunder? (No, it speaks to us gently like a beautiful sunrise.)

3) Does the still small voice shake us like a big earthquake? (No, it speaks to us carefully, like when the wind moves the clouds through the sky.)

📖 SCRIPTURE:

Read the following scriptures and discuss the questions that follow.

[D&C 85:6]

Yea, thus saith the still small voice, which whispereth through and pierceth all things, and often times it maketh my bones to quake while it maketh manifest,

1) Who is speaking in this verse? (Joseph Smith.)

2) What do you think it means for something to "whisper through" us? (Discuss.)

3) Why do you think Joseph Smith said the spirit sometimes makes his bones quake? (Discuss.)

[1 Nephi 17:45]

45 Ye are swift to do iniquity but slow to remember the Lord your God. Ye have seen an angel, and he spake unto you; yea, ye have heard his voice from time to time; and he hath spoken unto you in a still small voice, but ye were past feeling, that ye could not feel his words;

1) Who is speaking in this verse? *(Nephi is speaking to his brothers when they wouldn't help him build a ship.)*

2) Did Nephi's brothers hear the Lord when He spoke to them in a still small voice? *(No this did not feel His words.)*

3) Why didn't they feel the Lord's words when the Spirit spoke to them? *(Because they were "past feeling.")*

4) What do you think it means to be "past feeling?" *(Discuss things like not paying attention, not listening carefully, ignoring the spirit, disobedience, etc.)*

[Helaman 5:30]

5 And it came to pass when they heard this voice, and beheld that it was not a voice of thunder, neither was it a voice of a great tumultuous noise, but behold, it was a still voice of perfect mildness, as if it had been a whisper, and it did pierce even to the very soul.

1) When the people heard a voice, was it like thunder? *(No.)*

2) When the people heard a voice, did it make a "great noise?" *(No.)*

3) What was the voice like? *(It was a still voice of perfect mildness, and it was like a whisper.)*

ACTIVITY PAGES:

[Pass out coloring page]

Invite Children to color the coloring page from the video. Use this time to discuss why it is important to listen for the still small voice.

♡ TESTIMONY:

Bear testimony of the truths found in the scriptures.

This page intentionally left blank.

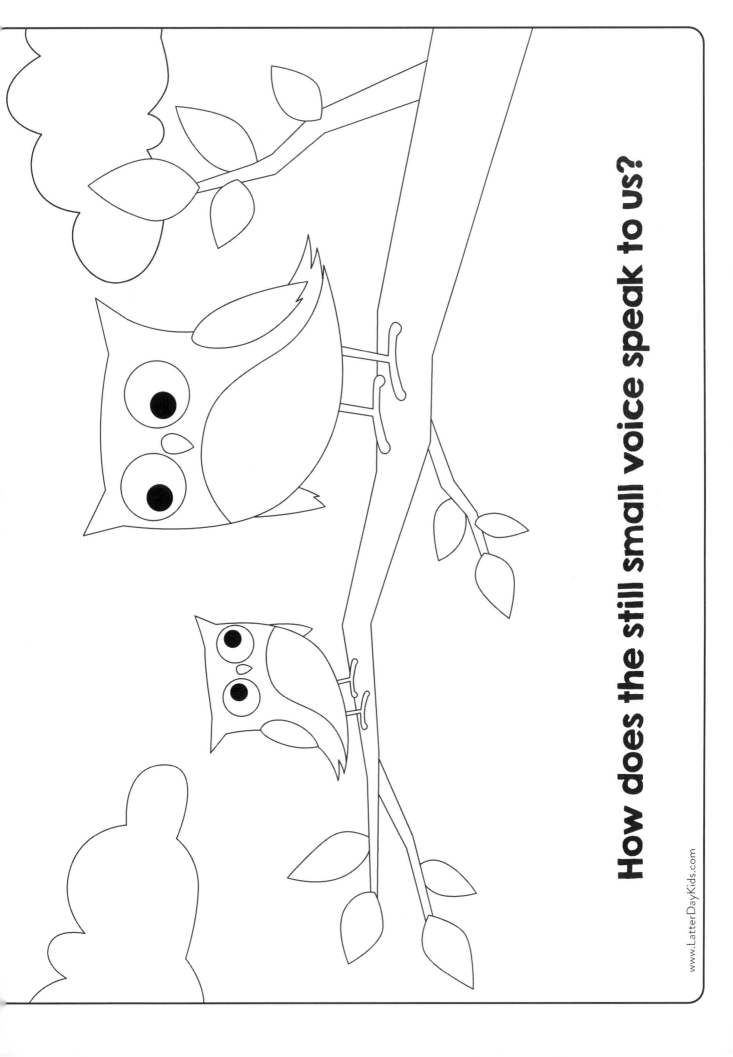

How does the still small voice speak to us?

This page intentionally left blank.

LATTER DAY
KIDS

Week 33: Aug 11 - 17

 D&C 88

 TOPIC | Draw Near Unto Me

♫ **OPENING SONG** "I Know My Father Lives"

✎ **PREPARATION:**

You will need a rope long enough to stretch across the room and an image of Jesus Christ. A thick rope (for pulling) would be ideal, but string or yarn will work as well. Tie each end of the rope to something sturdy on each end of the room (such as a door knob or a piece of furniture). The rope should be stretched across the room suspended in the air. Place the image of Jesus Christ at one end of the rope.

💬 INTRODUCTION ACTIVITY:

Invite the children to take turns "drawing near" to the Savior by pulling them themselves forward along the rope towards the image of Christ. Emphasize the pulling motion on the rope so that they will have a better understanding of what it means to "draw" near.

After you complete the activity, ask the following questions:

1) What do you think it means to "draw near" to the Savior? (Discuss.)

2) How did it feel to use your legs and your arms to draw near to Jesus instead of just using your legs? (Discuss.)

3) Imagine there was a big storm, and it was dark so you can't see. Then how would it feel to hold onto the rope? (Discuss.)

4) What are some things that we can hold onto when we are trying to draw near to Jesus

Christ in our hearts? *(Discuss things like family, the scriptures, the prophets, the Holy Ghost, the commandments, etc.)*

▶ VIDEO:

Now we are going to watch a video about a girl who wants to draw near to the Savior. The video will also show you three other things that Jesus told us we can do to be close to Him. See if you can remember the other three things!

[Watch Video: "Draw Near Unto Me | Animated Scripture Lesson for Kids"]

Discuss the following questions after watching the video:

1) What did the girl do to draw near to Jesus? *(She had to pull the rope to make the boat go across the lake.)*

2) Can you remember the other three things that Jesus has told us we can do to draw near unto Him? *(Seek and ye shall find, ask and ye shall receive, knock and it shall be opened unto you.)*

3) What did Jesus say He will do if we draw near unto Him? *(He will draw near unto us.)*

📖 SCRIPTURE:

Read the following scriptures and discuss the questions that follow.

[D&C 88:63]

Draw near unto me and I will draw near unto you; seek me diligently and ye shall find me; ask, and ye shall receive; knock, and it shall be opened unto you.

1) What did Jesus say will happen if we seek Him diligently? *(He said we will find Him.)*

2) Have you ever lost something before that you really wanted to find? How did it feel? *(Discuss.)*

3) What did Jesus say will happen if we seek Him diligently? *(We will find Him!)*

4) What are some things we can do to seek Jesus diligently? *(Discuss things like learning of Him, and trying to follow His example and keep His commandments.)*

[2 Nephi 32:4]

Wherefore, now after I have spoken these words, if ye cannot understand them it will be because ye ask not, neither do ye knock; wherefore, ye are not brought into the light, but must perish in the dark.

1) Who is speaking in this verse? *(Nephi is speaking to his brothers.)*

2) What is happening? *(Nephi is teaching his brothers about the Holy Ghost.)*

3) Why don't they understand what Nephi is teaching them? *(Because they don't "ask," and they don't "knock.")*

4) What do you think Nephi's brothers could do to "ask" and "knock?" *(Discuss things like studying the scriptures, pondering the words in the scriptures, and praying to ask Heavenly Father.)*

[Matthew 7:7-8]

Ask, and it shall be given you; seek, and ye shall find; knock, and it shall be opened unto you:
For every one that asketh receiveth; and he that seeketh findeth; and to him that knocketh it shall be opened.

1) What did Jesus tell us to do? *(Ask, seek, knock.)*

2) What did Jesus promise us? *(Everyone who asks will receive, everyone who seeks will find, and to everyone who knocks it will be opened.)*

 # ACTIVITY PAGES:

[Pass out coloring page]

Invite Children to color the coloring page from the video. Use this time to discuss what it means to draw near unto Jesus Christ, and what Jesus promised He will do if we draw near unto Him.

♡ TESTIMONY:

Bear testimony of the truths found in the scriptures.

217

This page intentionally left blank.

Draw near unto me and I will draw near unto you..."

This page intentionally left blank.

Week 34: Aug 18 - 24

 D&C 89-92

 TOPIC | The Word of Wisdom

 **OPENING SONG** "The Lord Gave Me a Temple"

✏ PREPARATION:

You will need three plastic water bottles. Fill one water bottle completely with water. Fill another one partially with water (about half way), and empty out the last water bottle completely.

💬 INTRODUCTION ACTIVITY:

Invite the children to take turns trying to do a bottle flip with the empty bottle. (*A bottle flip involves throwing a plastic bottle into the air so that it rotates, in an attempt to land it upright on its base or cap. If you're still unsure what a bottle flip is, look it up on the internet.*) Give them plenty of time to attempt this (it is nearly impossible). Next, invite the children to take turns trying to do a bottle flip with the bottle that is full of water (this is also nearly impossible). Now, invite the children to take turns trying to do a bottle flip with the partially filled water bottle. This will still take several attempts, but it is much easier to do! Allow them to keep trying until someone completes a successful bottle flip!

After you complete the activity, ask the following questions:

1) Did the bottle flip work very well when the bottle was empty? (*No.*)

2) Did the bottle flip work very well when the bottle was too full? (*No.*)

3) When did the bottle flip work the best? (*When there was just the right amount of water inside!*)

Explain: Did you know our bodies are kind of like these water bottles? If we eat and drink the right things, then we can be healthy and strong - just like when the bottle worked better when it had the right things inside. Heavenly Father created us, and in the scriptures He has taught us some things we can do to take care of our bodies. These special scriptures are called "The Word of Wisdom."

VIDEO:

Now we are going to watch a video about The Word of Wisdom. See if you can remember three things that Heavenly Father said are good for our body.

[Watch Video: "The Word of Wisdom | Animated Scripture Lesson for Kids"]

Discuss the following questions after watching the video:

1) What are some of the things that Heavenly Father said are good for the body? *(Discuss.)*

2) What are some of the things that Heavenly Father said are not good for the body? *(Discuss.)*

3) How are our bodies like an engine? *(Discuss.)*

4) Can you remember the blessings Heavenly Father said we would receive if we do these things and keep the commandments? *(We will be blessed with wisdom and knowledge, and we will run and not be weary and walk and not faint.)*

SCRIPTURE:

Read the following scriptures and discuss the questions that follow.

[D&C 89:18]

18 *And all saints who remember to keep and do these sayings, walking in obedience to the commandments, shall receive health in their navel and marrow to their bones;*

1) Who is speaking in this verse? *(The Lord.)*

2) What is our "navel?" *(Our belly button! It's where we got all of the vitamins and nutrients we needed from our mother before we were born!)*

3) What is bone marrow? (*Bone marrow is inside our bones, and bone marrow makes blood cells to help us fight infections and to be healthy.*)

4) What did the Lord promise us in this verse? (*That if we do these sayings, we shall receive health in our navel and marrow in our bones.*)

[D&C 89:19]

19 And shall find wisdom and great treasures of knowledge, even hidden treasures;

1) What did the Lord promise us in this verse? (*We will be blessed with wisdom and knowledge!*)

[D&C 89:20]

20 And shall run and not be weary, and shall walk and not faint.

1) What did the Lord promise us in this verse? (*Discuss things like energy, and not feeling tired or worn out.*)

2) Why do you think Heavenly Father wants us to know these things? (*Because He loves us and He wants us to have the blessings!*)

ACTIVITY PAGES:

[Pass out coloring pages]

Invite the children to color the coloring page from the video. Use this time to discuss the Word of Wisdom and the blessings that are promised through obedience to this law.

♡ TESTIMONY:

Bear testimony of the truths found in the scriptures.

This page intentionally left blank.

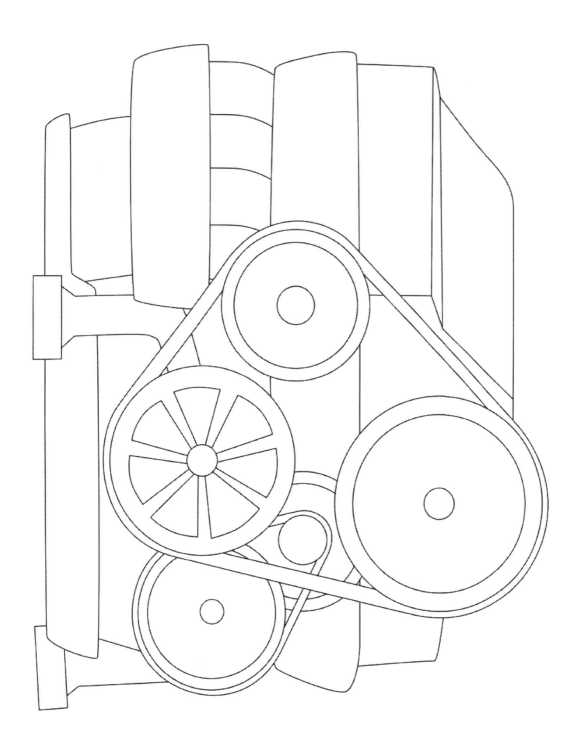

"...And shall run and not be weary, and shall walk and not faint."

-D&C 89:20

This page intentionally left blank.

LATTER DAY KIDS

Week 35: Aug 25 - 31

 D&C 93

 TOPIC | The Light of Truth

♪♪ **OPENING SONG** "The Iron Rod"

📝 **PREPARATION:**

You will need three plastic cups that are non-transparent, and you will need a ball or a small toy that fits inside the cups. Before you begin the lesson, turn the cups upside down and place the ball under one of the cups.

💬 **INTRODUCTION ACTIVITY:**

Direct the children's attention to the cups. Tell them that there is a ball underneath one of the cups. Then ask if they know which cup has a ball under it. Allow them to guess and encourage discussion, but don't reveal the truth yet!

Now pause the activity, and ask the following questions:

1) You have all guessed which cup is hiding the ball, but does anyone know the truth? (*None of the children know the truth. They can only guess!*)

2) What does it mean to know the truth? (*It means you are not guessing. You know which cup really has the ball!*)

3) Is there anyone in this room who knows the truth? (*You know the truth because you hid the ball!*)

4) How can you find out the truth? (*They could ask you to tell them, or they could ask you to look under the cups to find out for themselves!*)

227

Explain: Heavenly Father created us, and He is the creator of this world. He knows all things, and He is the source of all truth. We don't know all things, but if we can stay close to Him He will tell us the truth, and He will lead us to truth!

To conclude the activity, announce which cup has the ball, and then invite one of the children to lift the cup for the big reveal!

 # VIDEO:

Now we are going to watch a video about a little bird who is confused. She doesn't know what is true and what is not true! Let's watch and see what the other birds are telling her!

[Watch Video: "Gerdie the Birdie | A Story About Finding Truth"]

Discuss the following questions after watching the video:

1) What are some of the things that the first bird told Gerdie? (*Discuss.*)

2) What are some of the things that the second bird told Gerdie? (*Discuss.*)

3) Did Gerdie know which bird was telling the truth? (*No! She was very confused!*)

4) How does it feel when we don't know where to find the truth? (*It can be scary, confusing, and it doesn't feel good.*)

5) Does Heavenly Father want us to be scared and confused? (*No! He loves us and He wants us to find the truth and have peace!*)

6) What did Jesus teach us to do to receive truth from Him and from Heavenly Father? (*He said to search the scriptures, and pray to ask what is true.*)

 # SCRIPTURE:

Read the following scriptures and discuss the questions that follow.

[D&C 93:24]

And truth is knowledge of things as they are, and as they were, and as they are to come;

1) What does truth mean? *(It means knowing things as they really are.)*

2) Can we learn truth about things that have happened in the past? *(Yes!)*

3) Can we learn truth about things that will happen in the future? *(Yes!)*

4) Who knows the truth of all these things? *(Heavenly Father and Jesus Christ.)*

[John 18:37]

To this end was I born, and for this cause came I into the world, that I should bear witness unto the truth. Every one that is of the truth heareth my voice.

1) Who is speaking in this verse? *(Jesus Christ is speaking.)*

2) What did He say is one of the reasons He came into the world? *(To bear witness of the truth.)*

[Moroni 10:5]

And by the power of the Holy Ghost ye may know the truth of all things.

1) How can we learn the truth of all things? *(By the power of the Holy Ghost.)*

2) Who sends the Holy Ghost? *(Heavenly Father and Jesus Christ.)*

ACTIVITY PAGES:

[Pass out coloring page]

Invite the children to color the coloring page from the video, and to write "confusing" things in the word bubbles that the little bird is hearing. Encourage them to have fun and to use their imagination to make up silly things that the other birds might say! Use this time to discuss the importance of seeking truth the ways that Heavenly Father reveals truth to us.

♡ TESTIMONY:

Bear testimony of the truths found in the scriptures.

This page intentionally left blank.

This page intentionally left blank.

Week 36: Sept 1-7

 D&C 94-97

 TOPIC | The House of the Lord

 OPENING SONG "I Love to See the Temple"

✐ PREPARATION:

You will need a few sheets of aluminum foil and a lego person for each child. (If you don't have any lego persons available, you can use any other small toy figure).

💬 INTRODUCTION ACTIVITY:

Pass out a few sheets of aluminum foil and a lego person to each child. Then give the children the following instructions: "This lego person is you! The Lord has asked you to build a special place where He can talk to you and give you blessings and instructions! Use the aluminum foil to build this special and reverent place! You have five minutes to build it!"

When the children are finished, have them put the lego person inside their structure, and then have the children display their creations together in the front of the room.

After you complete the activity, ask the following questions:

1) How did you feel in your heart when you were building this special place where the Lord could talk to you? What were you thinking about? (*Discuss.*)

2) Has the Lord asked us to build places like this for real? (*Yes!*)

3) What are these places? (*Temples!*)

4) Why do you think the Lord has commanded us to build special places like this? *(So we can hear Him better, so we can think of Him instead of being distracted, so that we can protect that place and keep it special, etc..)*

Explain: Heavenly Father has commanded us to build special places where he can talk to us, teach us, and give us blessings. These places are called holy temples!

VIDEO:

Now we are going to watch a video about holy temples! While you are watching, see if you can find out why Heavenly Father wants us to build temples.

[Watch Video: "Why We Build Temples | Animated Scripture Lesson for Kids"]

Discuss the following questions after watching the video:

1) Why does Heavenly Father want us to build temples? *(Discuss.)*

2) Why did Moses and his people make a temple that was a tent and not a building? *(So they could take it with them when they were moving around.)*

3) What did Heavenly Father command Joseph Smith to do when the church was restored? *(Build a temple!)*

4) Do you know how many temples are on the earth today? *(There are currently 168 dedicated temples around the world!)*

SCRIPTURE:

Read the following scriptures and discuss the questions that follow.

[D&C 95:8]

Yea, verily I say unto you, I gave unto you a commandment that you should build a house, in the which house I design to endow those whom I have chosen with power from on high;

1) Who is the Lord talking to in this verse? *(Joseph Smith and the saints in Kirtland, Ohio.)*

2) Why did the Lord command the saints to build a temple? (*To give them blessings from on high!*)

[Luke 24:51-53]

And it came to pass, while he blessed them, he was parted from them, and carried up into heaven. And they worshipped him, and returned to Jerusalem with great joy: And were continually in the temple, praising and blessing God. Amen.

1) What happened in these verses? (*Jesus Christ blessed his disciples after He was resurrected, then He left and went up into heaven.*)

2) What did the disciples do after Jesus left and went up into heaven? (*They were continually in the temple!*)

3) Why do you think they spent a lot of time in the temple? (*Discuss.*)

[2 Nephi 5:16]

And I, Nephi, did build a temple; and I did construct it after the manner of the temple of Solomon save it were not built of so many precious things;

1) Who built a temple in this verse? (*Nephi built a temple!*)

2) Why do you think Nephi built a temple? (*He was commanded to. The Lord wanted them to have a special place where He could talk to Nephi and his people, and give them instructions and blessings.*)

ACTIVITY PAGES:

Pass out activity page]

Invite the children to cut out the rectangles and then assemble the image of the Salt Lake temple. Use this time to talk about why Heavenly Father commands us to build temples.

♡ TESTIMONY:

Bear testimony of truths found in scripture.

This page intentionally left blank.

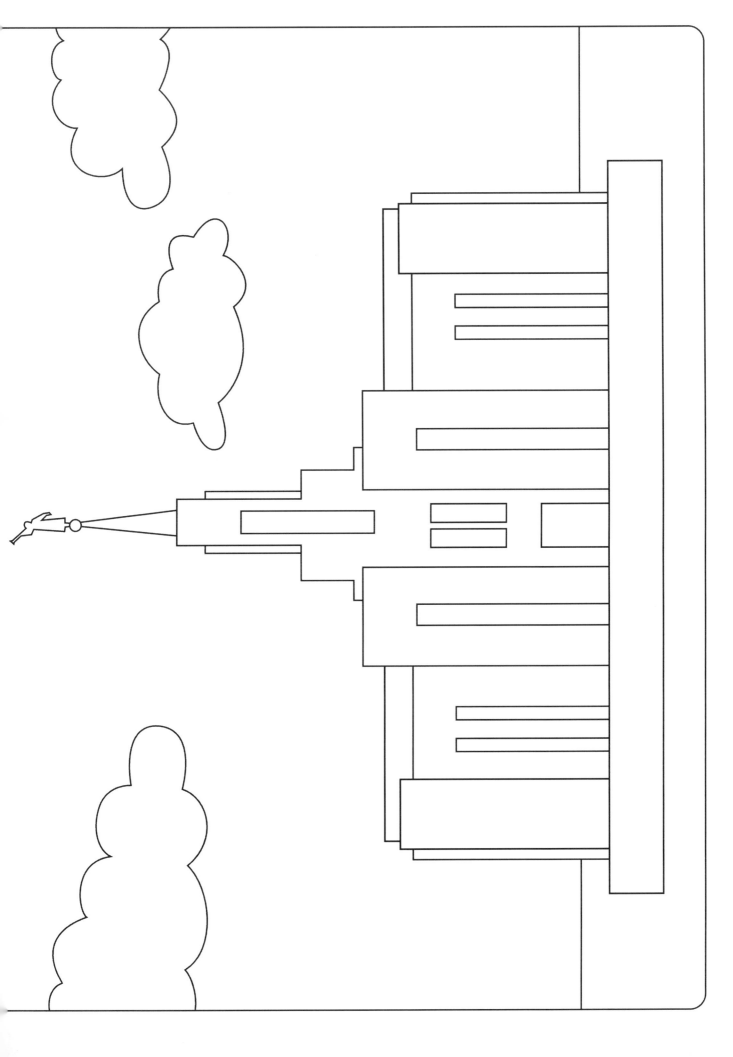

This page intentionally left blank.

Week 37: Sep 8 - 14

 D&C 98-101

 TOPIC | Be Still and Know that I Am God

OPENING SONG "If I Listen With My Heart"

✍ PREPARATION:

You will need a small cup of water (filled almost to the brim) and an image of Jesus Christ. Draw a heart on the cup, or tape a drawing of a heart to the cup. Place the cup of water and the image of Jesus Christ on the floor on the opposite side of the room.

▢ INTRODUCTION ACTIVITY:

Explain that the cup represents our hearts, and the water represents our faith in Jesus Crhist. Ask a volunteer to attempt to pick up the cup of water and bring it over to the image of Jesus Chirst without spilling any of the water. Allow the other children to do this activity one at a time until everyone has had a turn.

After you complete the activity, ask the following questions:

1) When you did this challenge, were you moving fast? Or slow? (*Discuss.*)

2) Were you wiggling? Or were you still and steady? (*Still!*)

3) Why were you slow, steady and still instead of rushing and wiggling? (*Because the water would have spilled!*)

4) What would have happened if you panicked and went too fast and tried to rush? (*Discuss.*)

Explain: When something goes wrong, or we feel worried, or upset, Heavenly Father has told us what to do. He said: "be still, and know that I am God." God is in control, and He loves us very much! He will take care of us if we will trust Him!

If we let our hearts get too worried, or if we rush or panic too much, then our faith can spill out of our hearts.

But, if we learn to keep our hearts calm, and steady, and still, (just like the cup of water) we can keep following Jesus Christ and our hearts can stay filled with faith!

VIDEO:

Now we are going to watch a video about learning to trust God instead of being fearful! Watch and see what these children were worried about and who was taking care of them.

[Watch Video: "Mother Knows What to Do | A Story About Trusting God"]

Discuss the following questions after watching the video:

1) What are some things that the children were worried about? (*The broken spoon, the lights, the lightning, and the empty cereal box.*)

2) Who was taking care of them? (*Their mother.*)

3) Did the children need to be worried? (*No, because Mother was watching over them.*)

4) What did the children learn to do at the end? (*They learned to trust their mother!*)

5) Why are we like the children? (*Because we are also learning to trust Heavenly Father to take care of us.*)

SCRIPTURE:

Read the following scriptures and discuss the questions that follow.

[D&C 101:16]

Therefore, let your hearts be comforted concerning Zion; for all flesh is in mine hands; be still and know that I am God.

1) What was happening when the Lord said this? (*The saints were being persecuted and forced to leave their homes.*)

2) What did the Lord tell them? (*He said to be still and know that I am God.*)

3) What does it mean to be still and know that I am God? (*It means not to be worried and to trust God.*)

[Matthew 8:24-25]

And, behold, there arose a great tempest in the sea, insomuch that the ship was covered with the waves: but he was asleep. And his disciples came to him, and awoke him, saying, Lord, save us: we perish.

1) What is happening in this verse? (*Jesus and His disciples were on a ship, and there was a great storm!*)

2) Who was asleep? (*Jesus was asleep.*)

3) What did the disciples do? (*They were worried, and they woke Jesus to ask Him to help.*)

[Matthew 8:26]

And he saith unto them, Why are ye fearful, O ye of little faith? Then he arose, and rebuked the winds and the sea; and there was a great calm.

1) What question did Jesus ask his disciples? (*He asked them why they were fearful.*)

2) What could they have done instead of being fearful? (*They could have trusted Heavenly Fathe to take care of them.*)

3) Does your heart ever feel like a storm? (*Discuss.*)

4) What did Heavenly Father tell us to do when we are worried and when we have a storm in our hearts? (*"Be still and know that I am God."*)

5) What does it mean to be still and know that I am God? (*It means not to be worried and to trust God.*

✎ ACTIVITY PAGES:

[Pass out activity page]

241

Invite the children to color the characters from the video. Fold along the dotted lines to make the mouths open and close! Have a discussion together about some things that you might feel worried about right now. (Use the characters to express your worries!)

Talk about Heavenly Father's love for you and His promises to you in the scriptures. Talk about what you can do to trust Him and to help your hearts be still and filled with faith.

 TESTIMONY:

Bear testimony of the truths found in the scriptures.

"O Lord, I have trusted in thee, and I will trust in thee forever."

-2 Nephi 4:34

fold

fold

This page intentionally left blank.

"O Lord, I have trusted in thee, and I will trust in thee forever."

-2 Nephi 4:34

fold

fold

This page intentionally left blank.

Week 38: Sep 15 - 21

 D&C 102-105

 TOPIC | I Can Be a Peacemaker

OPENING SONG "Tell Me the Stories of Jesus"

PREPARATION:

You will need an egg carton of any size filled with eggs.

INTRODUCTION ACTIVITY:

At the beginning of the lesson, give one egg to each child. Invite them to hold their egg carefully at their seat. Place the egg carton in the middle of the room. Tell the children that when you say "go," they should all walk to the egg carton and put their egg in one of the empty places in the carton and return to their seats. Once you have completed the activity, explain the following.

Today's lesson is about being a peacemaker. Jesus Christ taught us to be peacemakers and to spread peace everywhere we go. When you all put the eggs away, you were very careful and mindful of one another. That's a very important part of being a peacemaker!

Just like you were careful with each other when you were putting the eggs away, we should also be careful and mindful of one another at other times - like when we are playing together, when we are learning together, or when we are eating a meal together.

If we do this, we can help to spread peace and we can be a peacemaker!

▶ VIDEO:

Now we are going to watch a video about two truck drivers who want to use the same gas pump. Let's watch and see if one of the truck drivers decides to be a peacemaker!

[Watch Video: "A Tale of Two Trucks | A Story About Being a Peacemaker"]

Discuss the following questions after watching the video:

1) How did you feel in your heart when you were watching the truck drivers contending with one another? *(Discuss feelings the children might have felt, like worry, concern, fear, and uneasiness.)*

2) Do you think Heavenly Father wants us to feel this way? *(No.)*

3) What happened when the truck drivers both decided to be peacemakers? *(They both got gas, none of their trucks were broken, and they were happy!)*

4) What do you think would have happened if only one of the truck drivers decided to be a peacemaker? *(There still would have been peace!)*

SCRIPTURE:

Read the following scriptures and discuss the questions that follow.

[D&C 105:39]

And lift up an ensign of peace, and make a proclamation of peace unto the ends of the earth;

1) What is an ensign? *(It's something you hold up to show what you believe, like a flag or a banner.)*

2) How do you think we can show others how to be peacemakers? *(Discuss.)*

[3 Nephi 11:29]

For verily, verily I say unto you, he that hath the spirit of contention is not of me, but is of the devil, who is the father of contention, and he stirreth up the hearts of men to contend with anger, one with another.

1) Who is speaking in this verse? *(Jesus Christ is speaking.)*

2) Does Jesus Christ want us to contend with each other? *(No.)*

3) Why do you think Jesus Christ doesn't want us to contend with each other? *(Discuss what happens when we contend with each other.)*

[Mosiah 23:15]

Thus did Alma teach his people, that every man should love his neighbor as himself, that there should be no contention among them.

1) What did Alma teach his people? *(That they should love each other, and that there should be no contention among them.)*

2) What can we do to help make no contention among us? *(We can try to be a peacemaker!)*

 ## ACTIVITY PAGES:

[Pass out coloring page]

Invite the children to color the coloring page from the video. Invite them to practice being a peacemaker while they are coloring and sharing the crayons!

♡ TESTIMONY:

Bear testimony of the truths found in the scriptures.

This page intentionally left blank.

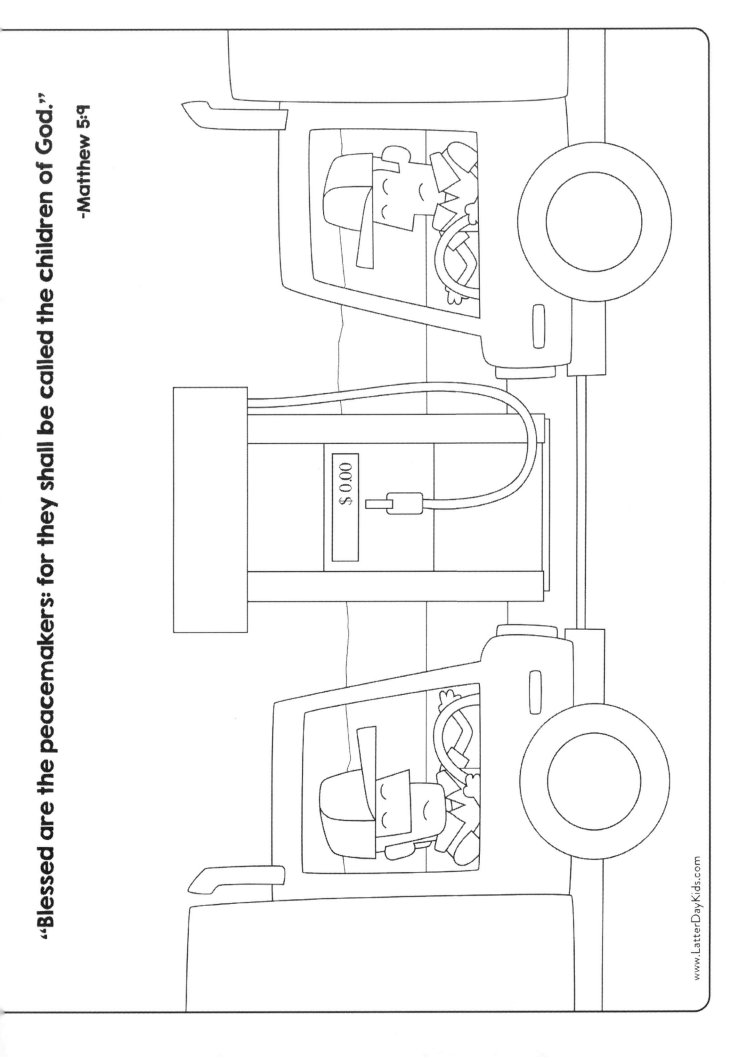

"Blessed are the peacemakers: for they shall be called the children of God."

-Matthew 5:9

$ 0.00

www.LatterDayKids.com

This page intentionally left blank.

Week 39: Sep 22 - 28

 D&C 106-108

 TOPIC | Strengthen Others in All Your Doings

♪ **OPENING SONG** "Nephi's Courage"

 **PREPARATION:**

You will need a stack of books, a small cup, and several sheets of printer paper.

💬 INTRODUCTION ACTIVITY:

Divide the books into two stacks and place a single sheet of paper on top to form a "bridge." Now place the cup on top of the paper to test the strength of the bridge. (The paper should bend, and the cup should fall between the books.) Now, invite the children to try to strengthen the bridge by folding the paper in different ways! Allow multiple attempts. See if they can find a way to make a bridge that is strong enough to hold the cup!

After you complete the activity, ask the following questions:

1) Was the bridge strong at first? Or was it weak? (*It was weak.*)

2) What did you do to make the bridge stronger? (*They folded the paper in different ways.*)

3) Do you think people need to be strong too, like the strong bridge? Why? (*Discuss some things that require strength, choosing the right, doing hard things, facing adversity, etc.*)

Explain: In the scriptures, Heavenly Father told us to strengthen one another. Just like we worked together to make the bridge stronger, we can also work together to help other people be stronger!

▶ VIDEO:

Now we are going to watch a video about strengthening others! See if you can remember some of the things we can do to strengthen others!

[Watch Video: "Strengthen One Another | Animated Scripture Lesson for Kids"]

Discuss the following questions after watching the video:

1) What can we do with physical strength? (*Discuss things like lifting heavy things, running fast, jumping high, etc.*)

2) What can we do with spiritual strength? (*We can live with greater faith, and we can keep the commandments even when it is hard to do.*)

3) What are some things we can do to strengthen others? (*Say nice things, help them feel the Holy Ghost, set an example, pray for them, etc.*)

📖 SCRIPTURE:

Read the following scriptures and discuss the questions that follow.

[D&C 108:7]

Therefore, strengthen your brethren in all your conversation, in all your prayers, in all your exhortations, and in all your doings.

1) What is the Lord asking us to do in this verse? (*He is asking us to strengthen others.*)

2) What are some ways we can strengthen others? (*In our conversation, in our prayers, and in all our doings.*)

[Mosiah 24:15]

And now it came to pass that the burdens which were laid upon Alma and his brethren were made light; yea, the Lord did strengthen them that they could bear up their burdens with ease, and they did submit cheerfully and with patience to all the will of the Lord.

1) Did the Lord take away the burdens that were hard for Alma and his brethren? (No.)

2) What did the Lord do to help them? (He strengthened them, so that they could bear their burdens with ease!)

3) Why do you think the Lord didn't take away their burdens? (Discuss.)

[Phillipians 4:13]

I can do all things through Christ which strengtheneth me.

1) Who is speaking in this verse? (The apostle Paul is speaking.)

2) Where does Paul get his strength? (Through Jesus Christ!)

3) How can we help others to be stronger like Paul? (We can help them come unto Jesus Christ.)

ACTIVITY PAGES:

[Pass out activity pages]

Invite the children to color the scene from the video and assemble the spinner by following the directions. Use this time to talk about things that you can do to help strengthen others.

♡ TESTIMONY:

Bear testimony of the truths found in the scriptures.

This page intentionally left blank.

Directions:

1. Print on cardstock for best results.
2. Color the girl and the weights!
3. Cut out the shape next to the girl on the dotted line.
2. Cut out the rotating disc on the dotted line.
4. Fasten the rotating disc behind the girl with a brad (make sure to line up the center of the circle with the dot on the girl's forehead!!).
5. Spin the rotating disc to reveal the different size weights!

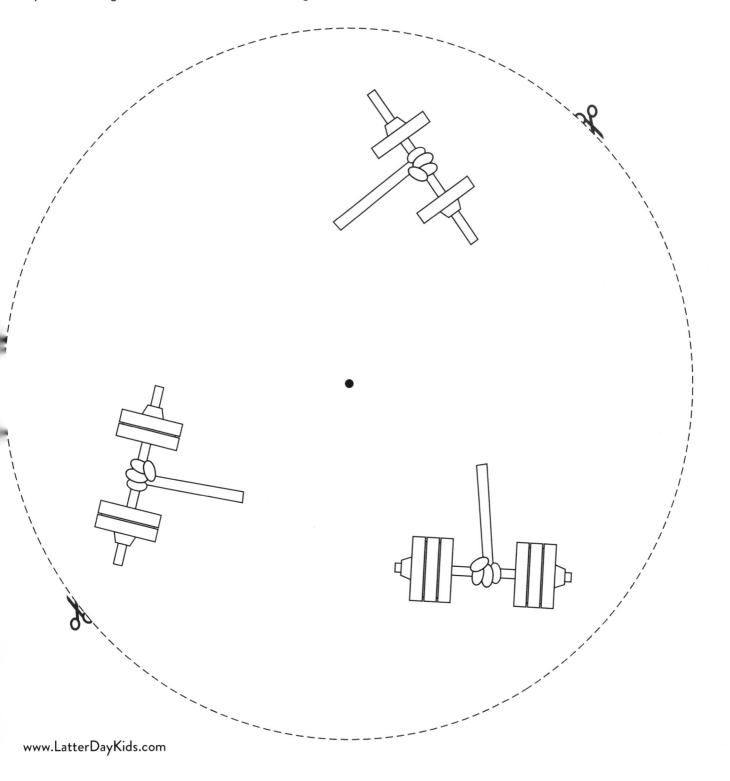

www.LatterDayKids.com

This page intentionally left blank.

"Therefore, strengthen your brethren in all your conversation, in all your prayers, in all your exhortations, and in all your doings."

-D&C 108:7

This page intentionally left blank.

LATTER DAY
KIDS

Week 40: Sept 29 - Oct 5

 D&C 109-110

 TOPIC | The Restoration of Priesthood Keys

 **OPENING SONG** "I Feel My Savior's Love"

✎ PREPARATION:

You will need a key that opens something (like a door or a padlock), and you will also need 4 other keys that go to something else. Separate all the keys from your keychain so that they can be passed around and handled separately.

💬 INTRODUCTION ACTIVITY:

Hold up all of the keys, and explain that one of these keys opens a lock! The other keys don't work for this lock. Now, lay the keys on the ground or on the table. Let the children take turns trying the keys in the lock, one at a time, to find the key that works!

After completing the activity, discuss the following questions:

1) Could you open this lock without a key? *(No.)*

2) Could you open this lock with any of the keys? *(No.)*

3) What did you need to be able to open the lock? *(The correct key!)*

Explain:

Today we are going to talk about the priesthood keys! God gives us priesthood keys to help Him do his work on the earth. We need priesthood keys for lots of things, like performing baptisms, sealing our families together in the temple, and administering the sacrament. If we don't have the priesthood keys for these things, that means we don't have permission to "open that lock."

▶ VIDEO:

Say: "Now we are going to watch a video about the restoration of the priesthood keys! Watch and see if you can remember some of the people who God sent to visit Joseph Smith to give him priesthood keys."

[Watch Video: "The Restoration of Priesthood Keys | Animated Scripture Lesson for Kids"]

Discuss the following questions after watching the video:

1) Can you remember any of the people who God sent to visit Joseph Smith? *(John the Baptist, Peter, James, John, Moses, Elias, Elijah.)*

2) Why did God send those people to visit Joseph Smith? *(To give him priesthood keys.)*

3) Who else received these priesthood keys with Joseph Smith? *(Oliver Cowdrey.)*

SCRIPTURE:

Read the following scriptures and discuss the questions that follow.

[D&C 110:16]

Therefore, the keys of this dispensation are committed into your hands; and by this ye may know that the great and dreadful day of the Lord is near, even at the doors.

1) Who is speaking in this verse? *(The Prophet Elijah is speaking.)*

2) Who sent Elijah? *(The Lord.)*

3) What did He say? *(That the priesthood keys were given to Joseph Smith.)*

[Matthew 16:19]

And I will give unto thee the keys of the kingdom of heaven: and whatsoever thou shalt bind on earth shall be bound in heaven: and whatsoever thou shalt loose on earth shall be loosed in heaven.

1) Who is speaking in this verse? *(Jesus Christ is speaking.)*

2) Do you know who he is speaking to? *(To His Apostle Peter.)*

[D&C 13:1]

Upon you my fellow servants, in the name of Messiah I confer the Priesthood of Aaron, which holds the keys of the ministering of angels, and of the gospel of repentance, and of baptism by immersion for the remission of sins...

1) Who is speaking in this verse? *(This is when John the Baptist appeared to Joseph Smith and Oliver Cowdrey.)*

2) What keys did John the Baptist give them? *(Ministering of angels, repentance, baptism.)*

 ## ACTIVITY PAGES:

[Pass out activity pages]

Invite the children to color the scene from the video! Use this time to talk about the restoration of the keys of the priesthood, and the importance of priesthood authority.

♡ TESTIMONY:

Bear testimony of the truths found in the scriptures.

This page intentionally left blank.

"Therefore, the keys of this dispensation are committed into your hands..."

-D&C 110:16

www.LatterDayKids.com

This page intentionally left blank.

Week 41: Oct 6 - 12

 D&C 111-114

TOPIC | Humility

OPENING SONG "He Sent His Son"

✒ PREPARATION:

You will need two seeds of any type. You will also need two pieces of paper. Write the word "humble" at the top of one paper, and write the word "not humble" at the top of the other paper.

💬 INTRODUCTION ACTIVITY:

Place the papers side by side on a table or on the floor. Place one seed on the "humble" paper, and place the other seed on the "not humble" paper.

Ask the children if the seeds can grow all by themselves, or if there are some other things that the seeds need. Each time the children think of something that the seed needs (soil, sunlight, water, someone to pull weeds, etc.), draw it on the "humble" paper! Explain that the other seed isn't humble, and it doesn't think it needs any help to grow. It just says no thanks!

1) Can we learn and grow by ourselves? Or do we need some help from Heavenly Father? (We need help from Heavenly Father, just like the seeds!)

2) What are some things that we need in order to learn and grow? (Discuss.)

3) What do you think we will do if we are like the humble seed? (We will receive blessings and commandments from Heavenly Father, and we will be thankful!)

4) What do you think we will do if we are like the "not humble" seed? (We might reject blessings from Heavenly Father, and we might not be thankful.)

▶ VIDEO:

Now we are going to watch a video about a humble bumble bee! Watch and see when the bumble bee decides to be humble!

[Watch Video: "The Humble Bumble Bee | Animated Scripture Lesson for Kids"]

Discuss the following questions after watching the video:

1) When did the bumble bee decide to be humble? *(When it couldn't kick the soccer ball.)*

2) What would have happened if the bumble bee was humble at the beginning? *(It would have learned how to kick the ball sooner.)*

3) Do you think we will learn more from Heavenly Father if we are humble? Or if we are not humble? *(We will learn more from Heavenly Father if we are humble.)*

📖 SCRIPTURE:

Read the following scriptures and discuss the questions that follow.

[D&C 112:10]

Be thou humble; and the Lord thy God shall lead thee by the hand, and give thee answer to thy prayers.

1) What did the Lord promise if we are humble? *(The Lord promised to lead us by the hand, and give us answers to our prayers.)*

2) Can the Lord lead us if we are not humble? *(No.)*

3) Why can't He lead us if we are not humble? *(Discuss.)*

[James 4:10]

Humble yourselves in the sight of the Lord, and he shall lift you up.

1) What can the Lord do if we will humble ourselves? *(He will lift us up!)*

2) Do you think it is hard to be humble sometimes? Why? *(Discuss.)*

[Alma 13:13]

And now, my brethren, I would that ye should humble yourselves before God, and bring forth fruit meet for repentance, that ye may also enter into that rest.

1) What is this scripture telling us to do? *(To be humble and to repent.)*

2) Why do we need to be humble to repent? *(If we are humble, then we will be willing to listen to God and receive His commandments.)*

 ## ACTIVITY PAGES:

[Pass out activity pages]

Invite the children to color the scene from the video. Use this time to talk about what it means to humble ourselves.

♡ TESTIMONY:

Bear testimony of the truths found in the scriptures.

This page intentionally left blank.

"Be thou humble; and the Lord thy God shall lead thee by the hand, and give thee answer to thy prayers."

-D&C 112:10

www.LatterDayKids.com

This page intentionally left blank.

Week 42: Oct 13 - 19

 D&C 115-120

 TOPIC | The Law of Tithing

 ♪ **OPENING SONG** | "Keep the Commandments"

✐ **PREPARATION:**

You will need a small cup, a bag of rice, and a large bowl.

💬 **INTRODUCTION ACTIVITY:**

Invite one of the children to hold the cup to receive God's "blessings" in the cup. Invite everyone to take turns naming specific blessings that they have received from Heavenly Father. Each time someone names a blessing, drop a single grain of rice into the cup. After everyone has had a turn to name a few blessings, read the following verse.

*"Bring ye all the tithes into the storehouse, that there may be meat in my house; and prove me now herewith, saith the Lord of Hosts, if I will not open you the windows of heaven, and pour you out a blessing that **there shall not be room enough to receive it**." (Emphasis added.)*

-3 Nephi 24:10

Now ask the following question:

1) What do you think it would look like if Heavenly Father gave us blessings so great that we didn't have enough room to receive it? *(Discuss.)*

2) Does Heavenly Father ever break a promise? *(No.)*

3) Ask "Do you know what the law of tithing is?" (*Discuss. If needed, explain that tithing is when we offer one tenth of our increase to God.*)

Now place the bowl under the cup (to catch the excess) and slowly pour all of the rice into the cup so that the children can watch the cup fill and continuously overflow.

Explain: Today we are going to learn about God's law of tithing! When we are baptized, the law of tithing is one of the commandments that we promise to keep. And God has promised us great blessings when we keep this law.

▶️ VIDEO:

Say: "Now we are going to watch a video about tithing! See if you can remember some of the things that our tithing money is used for."

[Watch Video: "What is Tithing? | Animated Scripture Lesson for Kids"]

Discuss the following questions after watching the video:

1) What does the word tithing mean? (*It means one tenth, or one out of ten.*)

2) Do you remember any of the things that our tithing funds will be used for? (*Discuss examples from the video.*)

3) Do you think it will always be easy for us to pay our tithing? (*No, sometimes it will be a sacrifice.*)

4) Do you think Heavenly Father will take our tithing from us, or do you think He will let us choose? (*He will let us choose.*)

5) Why do you think He will let us choose? (*Discuss.*)

SCRIPTURE:

Read the following scriptures and discuss the questions that follow.

[Read D&C 119:3-4]

And this shall be the beginning of the tithing of my people. And after that, those who have thus been tithed shall pay one-tenth of all their interest annually; and this shall be a standing law unto them forever, for my holy priesthood, saith the Lord.

1) How much has the Lord commanded us to pay in tithing? (*One tenth, or one out of ten.*)

2) What does the word "interest" mean? (*Discuss.*)

[Read Alma 13:15]

15 And it was this same Melchizedek to whom Abraham paid tithes; yea, even our father Abraham paid tithes of one-tenth part of all he possessed.

1) Who paid tithing in this verse? (*Abraham paid his tithes.*)

2) How much did Abraham give to God? (*One tenth.*)

[Read 3 Nephi 24:10]

Bring ye all the tithes into the storehouse, that there may be meat in my house; and prove me now herewith, saith the Lord of Hosts, if I will not open you the windows of heaven, and pour you out a blessing that there shall not be room enough to receive it.

1) Does the Lord break His promises? Or does He keep His promises? (*He always keeps His promises.*)

2) What did the Lord promise in this verse? (*He promised to open the windows of heaven and pour out a blessing.*)

3) If we pay our tithing, what does that mean? (*It means that we can have faith in that promise!*)

✏ ACTIVITY PAGES:

[Pass out the Coloring Page]

Invite the children to color and cut out the pretend money. Have them practice calculating one tenth using the pretend money. You could also have children fill the cup (from the activity at the beginning of the lesson) to represent blessings from Heavenly Father. Then take the tithing back out of the cup!

♡ TESTIMONY:

Bear testimony of the truths found in the scriptures.

This page intentionally left blank.

Tithing = 1 out of 10

This page intentionally left blank.

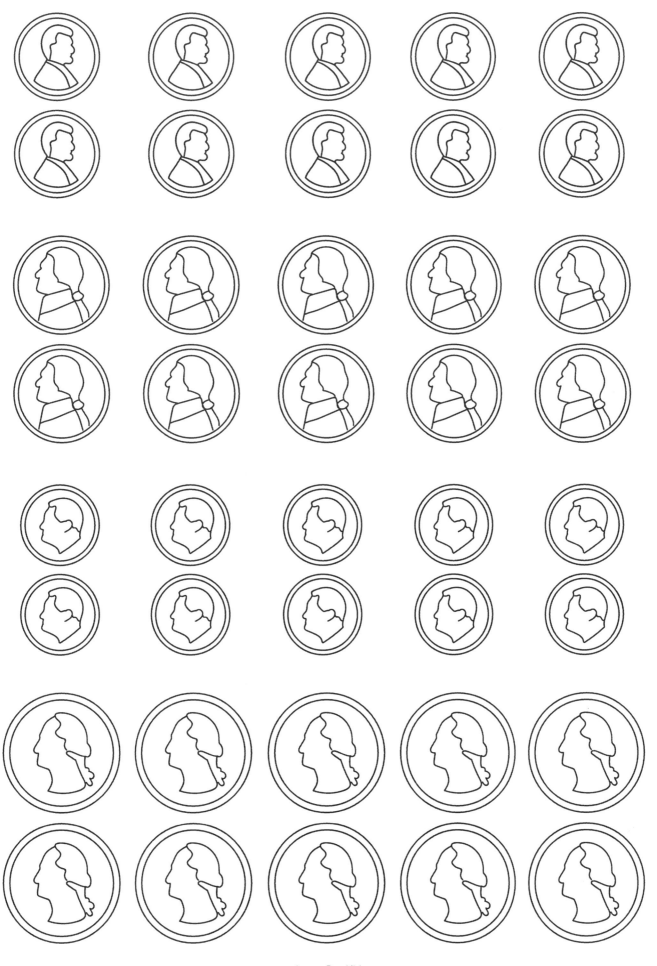

This page intentionally left blank.

Week 43: Oct 20 - 26

 D&C 121-123

 TOPIC | Our Trials Can Be For Our Good

🎵 **OPENING SONG** "I'm Trying to Be Like Jesus"

📝 **PREPARATION:**

You will need several sheets of printer paper.

💬 **INTRODUCTION ACTIVITY:**

Hold up the sheet of paper, and tell the children that you are going to make a paper airplane. Explain that in order to make the paper airplane, you are going to have to bend the paper. Explain that bending the paper is kind of like when we have trials in our lives. Each time you make a new fold, have the children say "ouch" together.

Now pass out a sheet of paper to each child and invite them to make their own paper airplanes. Display all the finished airplanes together where everyone can see them, then discuss the following questions.

1) What did the paper become? (*A paper airplane!*)

2) Why did the paper need folds in it? (*So it could become an airplane!*)

3) What does Heavenly Father want us to become? (*He wants us to be like Him and have a fullness of joy!*)

4) Why do we need trials? (*Because they help us to become more like Heavenly Father.*)

Explain: A trial is when we have to experience something that is hard for us. A trial might make us feel sad, or it might make us feel angry, or hurt, or scared. Our trials can be very hard right now, but later, if we have faith in Jesus Christ, we will see that our trials can be for our good, like the folds in the paper airplane. And Heavenly Father will help us in our trials.

VIDEO:

Now we are going to watch a video about a stonecutter! Watch and see if you can remember some of the things that the stonecutter was making!

[Watch Video: "The Stonecutter | A Story about Trials and Adversity"]

Discuss the following questions after watching the video:

1) What are some of the things the stonecutter was making? (*A duck, a digger, a grandmother, a bumble bee, and some children!*)

2) Why did the rocks have to have pieces broken off? (*So that they could become something new!*)

3) Who is the stonecutter kind of like? (*Heavenly Father.*)

4) What does Heavenly Father want to help us become? (*He wants us to learn and grow and become like Him!*)

SCRIPTURE:

Read the following scriptures and discuss the questions that follow.

[D&C 121:7]

My son, peace be unto thy soul; thine adversity and thine afflictions shall be but a small moment;

1) How long will we live after we are resurrected? (*Forever!*)

2) How long will our trials last? (*A small moment. Not very long compared to forever!*)

[D&C 121:9]

Thy friends do stand by thee, and they shall hail thee again with warm hearts and friendly hands.

1) Who can help us in our trials? (*Our friends can help us, and we can help others!*)

[Mosiah 3:7]

And lo, he shall suffer temptations, and pain of body, hunger, thirst, and fatigue, even more than man can suffer, except it be unto death; for behold, blood cometh from every pore, so great shall be his anguish for the wickedness and the abominations of his people.

1) Who is this scripture talking about? (*Jesus Christ.*)

2) Did Jesus Christ experience trials? (*Yes.*)

3) Why did Jesus Christ go through trials and suffering? (*Discuss.*)

ACTIVITY PAGES:

[Pass out coloring page]

Invite the children to color the scene from the video. Use this time to talk about trials, and how trials can be for our good.

♡ TESTIMONY:

Bear testimony of the truths found in the scriptures.

This page intentionally left blank.

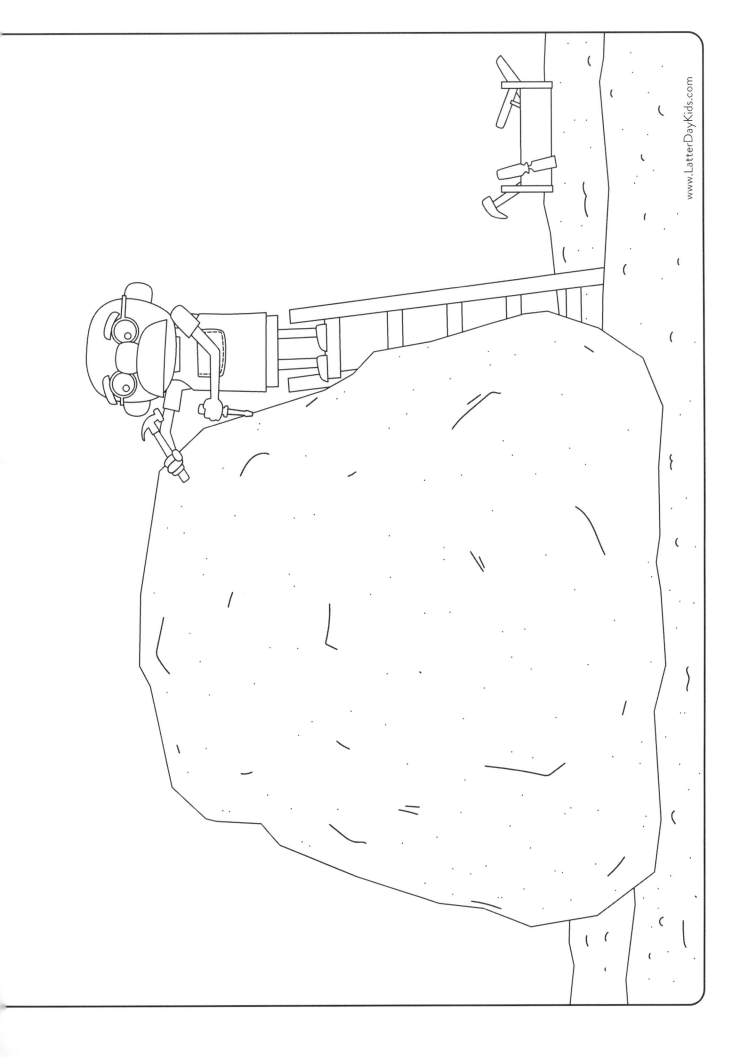

This page intentionally left blank.

Week 44: Oct 27 - Nov 2

 D&C 124

 TOPIC | Temple Ordinances

 OPENING SONG "I Love to See the Temple"

✎ PREPARATION:

Invite children to stand. Tell them that they will now be asked to point in several different directions and to follow the instructions to the best of their ability.

Point down! Use both arms and keep your arms straight. Reach as low as you can!

Now point to the right! Keep your arms straight. You can lean with your body too if you want. Reach over as far as you can.

Now point to the left! Keep your arms straight. You can lean with your body too if you want. Reach over as far as you can.

Now point up. Use both arms together and reach up as high as you can!

Ask the following question:

When you were pointing, which way makes you think of Heavenly Father the most? *(Discuss)*

Display a picture of a temple with a spire. Explain that Heavenly Father has commanded us to build temples on the earth, and that temples help us to grow closer to Heavenly Father. Even if we just look at a temple it makes us think about Heavenly Father right away, because it is pointing up!

▶ VIDEO:

Say: "Do you know what's inside a temple? We're going to watch a video that will show you six things that we can find inside a temple! Let's see how many you can remember!"

[Watch Video: "What's Inside the Temple? | Animated Children's Video"]

Discuss the following questions after watching the video:

1) Can you remember all six things that we can find inside a temple? *(Discuss)*

2) What do we do at the recommended desk? *(Discuss)*

3) Why do we need a recommend to enter the temple? *(To make sure we are ready)*

4) What do we do in the locker room? *(Discuss)*

5) Why do we wear white clothes in the temple? *(Discuss symbolism)*

6) What do we do in the baptistry? *(Discuss)*

7) What do we do in the endowment room? *(Learn, make promises, receive ordinances)*

8) What do we do in the sealing room? *(Families are sealed together forever)*

9) What do we do in the celestial room? *(Think about being with Heavenly Father and Jesus Christ, feel peace, pray quietly)*

📖 SCRIPTURE:

Read the following scriptures together and discuss the questions that follow. Invite children to put their hands together like a spire while they listen to the verse.

[Read 2 Nephi 12:2]

1) What is the "Mountain of the Lord's House?" *(Temple)*

2) Whose house is this temple? *(The Lord/Heavenly Father)*

3) Who will go to the temple? *(All nations)*

[Read 2 Nephi 12:3]

1) Whose ways do we learn about in the temple? *(Heavenly Father/Jesus Christ)*

2) What do you think it means to walk in His paths? *(Discuss)*

✎ ACTIVITY:

[Pass out activity pages]

Invite children to color the Salt Lake Temple coloring page! You can lead a discussion about what is inside the temple as they color.

♡ TESTIMONY:

Bear testimony of the truths found in the scriptures.

This page intentionally left blank.

This page intentionally left blank.

Week 45: Nov 3 - 9

 D&C 125-128

 TOPIC | I Can Care for My Family

 OPENING SONG "If the Savior Stood Beside Me"

✎ PREPARATION:

You will need to gather several stuffed animals that show different personalities.

💬 INTRODUCTION ACTIVITY:

Set up the stuffed animals in a row so that they are all "sitting" next to each other facing the children. Invite children to look closely at each of the animals one at a time, and then discuss the following questions for each animal:

1) What do you think this stuffed animal might be feeling right now? (*Happy? Sad? Hungry?*)

2) What makes this stuffed animal special? (*Discuss.*)

3) What kind of things do you think this stuffed animal likes to do? (*Discuss.*)

4) Imagine it's this animal's birthday and we want to help this stuffed animal to have a great day. What is something we could do that would make this stuffed animal really happy? (*Discuss.*)

Explain: Jesus Christ taught us to love and serve one another. Just like we thought of some ways to serve these stuffed animals, we can also think of ways to serve the people all around us! And, we can serve other people anytime! (Even if it is not their birthday!)

▶ VIDEO:

Say: "Now we are going to watch a video about serving others! The children in this video are little, but they find big ways to help their families! Let's see what ideas they think of!"

[Watch Video: "I'm So Little, What Can I Do? | A Story About Serving Others"]

Discuss the following questions after watching the video:

1) What are some things that the children did to help their families? (*Played with a sad little sister, helped find lost shoes, did dishes, made paper snowflakes.*)

2) Did they all do the same thing? Or did they do different things? (*They all thought of different things to do!*)

3) How do you think each child knew what to do? (*They watched the people around them to see what they needed.*)

📖 SCRIPTURE:

Read the following scripture together and discuss the questions that follow.

[Read D&C 126:3]

I therefore command you to send my word abroad, and take especial care of your family from this time, henceforth and forever. Amen.

1) Who is the Lord speaking to in this verse? (*Brigham Young.*)

2) What did the Lord tell Brigham Young to do? (*To take care of his family.*)

3) Can children also help take care of their families? What can they do? (*Discuss.*)

[Read John 13:34-35]

A new commandment I give unto you, That ye love one another; as I have loved you, that ye also love one another. By this shall all men know that ye are my disciples, if ye have love one to another.

1) What is the Lord commanding us to do in this verse? (*To love one another.*)

2) How will people know that we follow Jesus Christ? *(When they see that we love one another.)*

3) How can we show that we have love for someone? *(Discuss.)*

[Read Mosiah 2:17]

And behold, I tell you these things that ye may learn wisdom; that ye may learn that when ye are in the service of your fellow beings ye are only in the service of your God.

1) If we want to serve God, what is something we can do? *(Serve one another!)*

2) Why do you think God wants us to serve each other? *(Discuss.)*

3) How do we know what we can do to serve others? *(By watching other people to see what they need!)*

ACTIVITY PAGES:

[Pass out the coloring page]

Invite children to color the scene from the video. Use this time to talk about loving and serving others.

♡ TESTIMONY:

Bear testimony of the truths found in the scriptures.

This page intentionally left blank.

This page intentionally left blank.

LATTER DAY KIDS

Week 46: Nov 10 - 16

 D&C 129-132

 TOPIC | Obedience

 **OPENING SONG** "Choose the Right"

✏️ PREPARATION:

Collect several hard cover books to use as dominoes! The more the better! You will also need a marker and two sheets of printer paper.

💬 INTRODUCTION ACTIVITY:

Draw a happy face on one paper, and draw a sad face on the other paper. Stand the books on end to form two separate rows of "dominoes." Place the happy face at the end of one row, and place the sad face at the end of the other row. Hint: The books will balance more easily if you open them slightly!

After you have set up the activity, point to the first book in the "happy" row and ask:

1) What do you think will happen if we tip over this book? (*The books will knock each other over all the way to the happy face!*)

Now, point to the first book in the "sad" row and ask:

1) What do you think will happen if we tip over this book? (The books will knock each other over all the way to the sad face!

Explain that when God gives us a commandment, we have a choice to make. Choosing to obey a commandment from Heavenly Father leads to happiness. Sometimes now, sometimes later. (Tip over the first book to start the chain reaction.)

Choosing not to obey a commandment from Heavenly Father leads to unhappiness. Sometimes now, sometimes later. (Tip over the first book in the other row to start the chain reaction.)

VIDEO:

Say: "Now we are going to watch a video about a girl who is baking cookies with a recipe from a recipe book! Let's watch and see if she decides to follow the recipe, or if she decides to ignore the recipe!"

[Watch Video: "Just Follow the Recipe! | A Story About Obedience"]

Discuss the following questions after watching the video:

1) Did the girl choose to follow the recipe? (*No!*)

2) What happened when she didn't follow the recipe? (*The cookies didn't turn out right!*)

3) Why does Heavenly Father give us commandments? (*He wants us to be happy, and He knows the recipe!*)

4) What will happen if we follow the recipe? (*We will be happy!*)

5) Can you think of some things that Heavenly Father has commanded us to do? (*Discuss.*)

SCRIPTURE:

Read the following scripture together and discuss the questions that follow.

[Read D&C 130:20]

And when we obtain any blessing from God, it is by obedience to that law upon which it is predicated.

1) How can we obtain blessings from God? (*By obedience to the laws He gives us.*)

2) What do you think will happen if we choose not to obey God's laws? (*We will not receive the blessing.*)

[Read 2 Nephi 31:7]

Know ye not that he was holy? But notwithstanding he being holy, he showeth unto the children of men that, according to the flesh he humbleth himself before the Father, and witnesseth unto the Father that he would be obedient unto him in keeping his commandments.

1) Who is this scripture talking about? *(Jesus Christ.)*

2) Did Jesus Christ obey Heavenly Father's Commandments? *(Yes!)*

[Read Mosiah 2:41]

And moreover, I would desire that ye should consider on the blessed and happy state of those that keep the commandments of God. For behold, they are blessed in all things, both temporal and spiritual; and if they hold out faithful to the end they are received into heaven, that thereby they may dwell with God in a state of never-ending happiness. O remember, remember that these things are true; for the Lord God hath spoken it.

1) If we choose to keep the commandments, what will be the result? *(We will be blessed in temporal and spiritual things, and we will be in a state of happiness!)*

2) Who said this the truth? *(The Lord God has spoken it!)*

✏ ACTIVITY PAGES:

[Pass out the coloring page]

Invite children to color the scene from the video. In the blank space, write or draw some things that Heavenly Father has commanded us to do! Use this time to talk about commandments found in the scriptures and the promised blessings.

♡ TESTIMONY:

Bear testimony of the truths found in the scriptures.

This page intentionally left blank.

This page intentionally left blank.

Week 47: Nov 17 - 23

 D&C 133-134

| **TOPIC** | Jesus Christ Will Come Again |

 OPENING SONG "When He Comes Again"

✎ PREPARATION:

You will need some metal paper clips, some toothpicks, and a magnet.

💬 INTRODUCTION ACTIVITY:

Align the toothpicks and the paperclips in a row on a table or a flat surface. Hold up the magnet, then discuss the following questions.

1) What do you think will happen if I hold this magnet near the paper clips? *(The paperclips will stick to the magnet!)*

2) What do you think will happen if I hold this magnet near the toothpicks? *(Nothing! The toothpicks will stay on the table.)*

3) Why will the paperclips go to the magnet? *(Because they are magnetic and they want to go to the magnet.)*

4) Why won't the toothpicks go to the magnet? *(Because wood is non-magnetic, so wood does not want to go to the magnet.)*

Explain that Jesus Christ will come again to the Earth. When He comes again, He won't He won't be a baby. He will come as a king with great power and glory! If we are prepared and we have turned our hearts to Him, we will have joy when we see Him, and we will want to go to Him when He gathers His saints! (Use the magnet to gather the paper clips!)

But if we are not prepared and if we have turned our hearts away from Him, we will be afraid and ashamed. We will want to hide from Him. (Use the magnet to show how the toothpicks reject the magnet and will not go to it.)

▶️ VIDEO:

Say: "Now we are going to watch a video about some children who are going on a field trip to the zoo! Some of them prepared for the trip, and some of them did not prepare. Let's watch and see what happens!"

[Watch Video: "The Field Trip | Preparing for The Second Coming"]

Discuss the following questions after watching the video:

1) What happened to the children who were prepared? *(They got on the bus and they went on the field trip.)*

2) What happened to the children who did not prepare? *(They missed the bus and they didn't get to go on the field trip.)*

3) Why didn't they prepare? *(They thought they had enough time, but the bus suddenly came when they weren't ready.)*

4) What is the bus a symbol of? *(It's a symbol of Jesus Christ's second coming.)*

5) What do we need to do to be prepared for Jesus Christ's second coming? *(Discuss things like studying the scriptures, strengthening our testimonies, sharing the gospel with others, and keeping the commandments.)*

6) Can we prepare really fast if He comes suddenly? Or do we need to prepare early? *(We need to prepare early.)*

📖 SCRIPTURE:

Read the following scripture together and discuss the questions that follow.

[Read D&C 133:10]

Yea, let the cry go forth among all people: Awake and arise and go forth to meet the Bridegroom; behold and lo, the Bridegroom cometh; go ye out to meet him. Prepare yourselves for the great day of the Lord.

    1) Who is the bridegroom? *(Jesus Christ is the bridegroom.)*

    2) What does this scripture tell us to do before the great day? *(To prepare!)*

[Read Matthew 24:44]

Therefore be ye also ready: for in such an hour as ye think not the Son of man cometh.

    1) When will Jesus Christ come? *(In a time that we "think not." It will be a surprise!)*

    2) What is this scripture telling us to do? *(To be ready!)*

[Read Matthew 16:27]

For the Son of man shall come in the glory of his Father with his angels; and then he shall reward every man according to his works.

    1) How will Jesus appear when He comes again? *(In the glory of His Father!)*

 ## ACTIVITY PAGES:

[Pass out the coloring page]

Invite children to color the scene from the video and complete the "Spiritual Lunch Bag" activity page. Use this time to talk about what the scriptures and prophets have told us to do to prepare for the second coming.

♡ TESTIMONY:

Bear testimony of the truths found in the scriptures.

This page intentionally left blank.

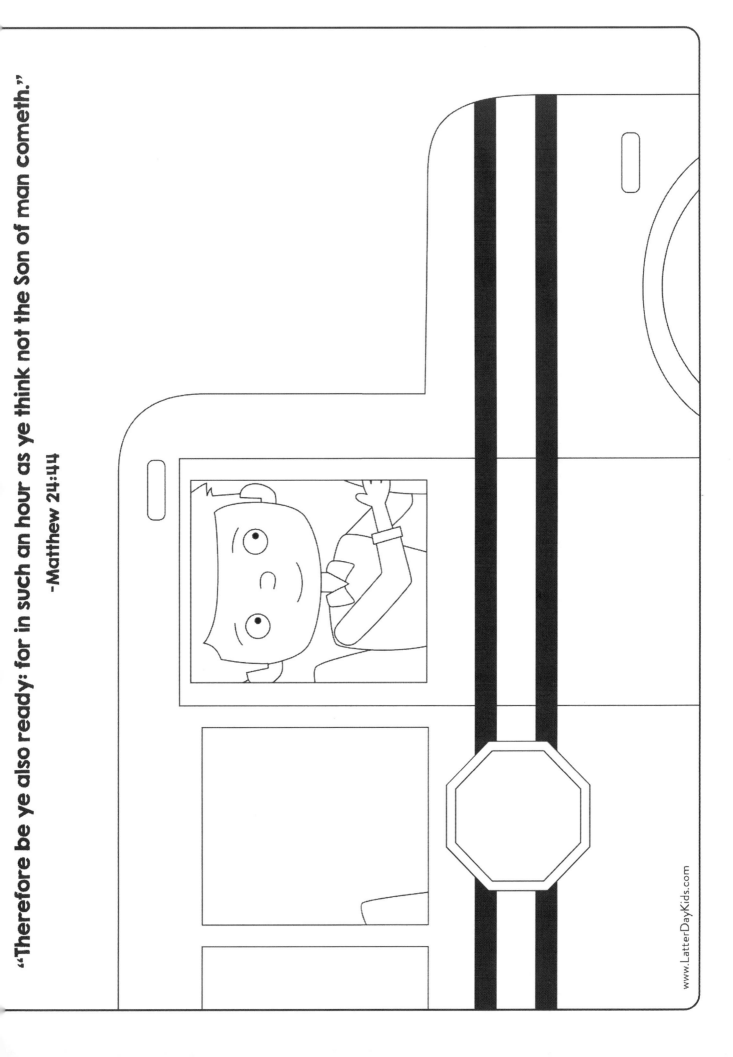

"Therefore be ye also ready: for in such an hour as ye think not the Son of man cometh."

-Matthew 24:44

www.LatterDayKids.com

This page intentionally left blank.

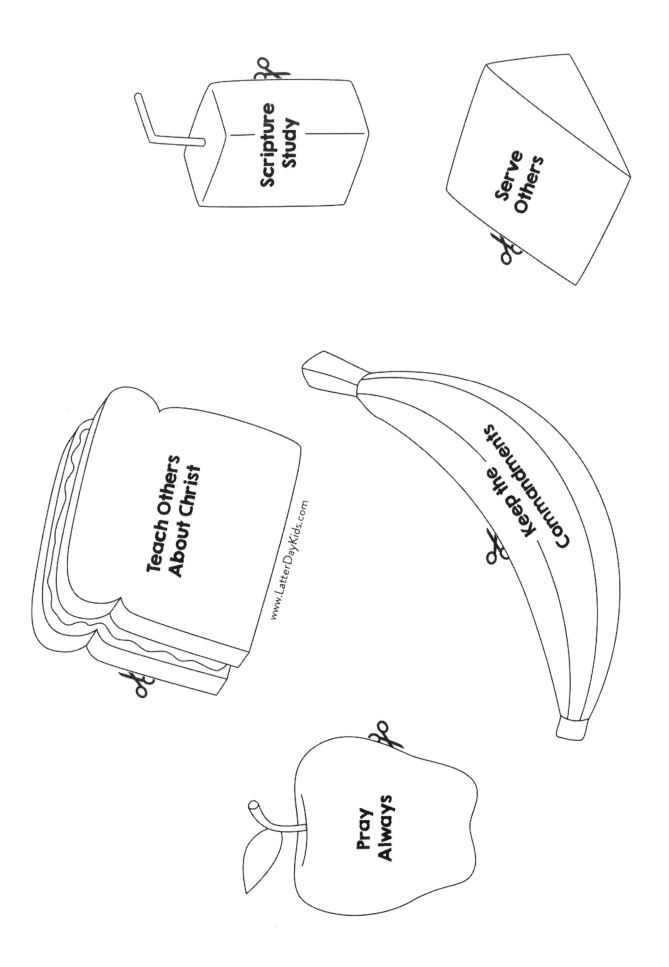

Scripture Study

Serve Others

Teach Others About Christ

www.LatterDayKids.com

Keep the Commandments

Pray Always

This page intentionally left blank.

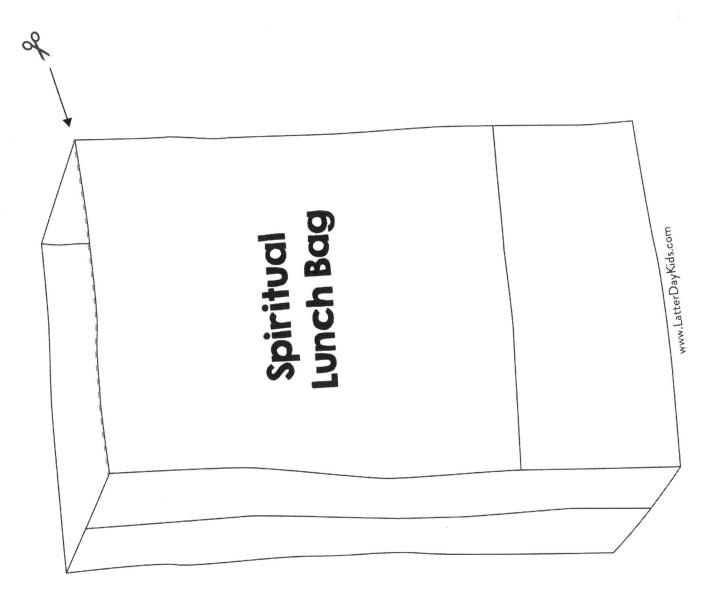

Prepare for His Coming!

1. Cut a slit in the bag along the dotted line.

2. Color and cut out the objects on the next page.

3. Pack your lunch by passing the objects through the slit into the bag!

Spiritual Lunch Bag

This page intentionally left blank.

LATTER DAY
KIDS

Week 48: Nov 24 - 30

📖 **D&C 135-136**

💡 **TOPIC** | Joseph Smith the Prophet

🎵 **OPENING SONG** "Praise to the Man"

✒️ **PREPARATION:**

You will need to print and cut out the "Joseph Smith" puzzle prior to the lesson.

💬 **INTRODUCTION ACTIVITY:**

Invite the children to work together in a group to assemble the Joseph Smith puzzle included in this lesson bundle.

Once the puzzle is completed, invite the children to return to their seats and ask the following questions:

1) Do you know who this is? (*Joseph Smith.*)

2) What do you know about Joseph Smith? (*Allow children to share what they know about Joseph Smith.*)

Explain: God called Joseph Smith to be a Prophet and to restore Jesus Christ's church to the earth in the latter days! Today, we are going to learn about Joseph Smith and some of the important things that God asked Joseph Smith to do.

▶️ **VIDEO:**

Say: "Now we are going to watch a video about Joseph Smith the prophet. See if you can remember something that Joseph Smith was called to do."

[Watch Video: "Joseph Smith the Prophet | Animated Scripture Lesson for Kids"]

Discuss the following questions after watching the video:

1) Why did Joseph Smith go into the woods to pray near his home? (*He wanted to know which church to join, and he read a scripture that said to ask God.*)

2) Can you remember some of the things that Joseph Smith did as the prophet of the restoration? (*He translated the Book of Mormon and got it printed, he organized the church, he restored the priesthood, and he restored the temple ordinances.*)

📖 SCRIPTURE:

Read the following scriptures and discuss the questions that follow.

[Read D&C 124:125]

I give unto you my servant Joseph to be a presiding elder over all my church, to be a translator, a revelator, a seer, and prophet.

1) Who is speaking in this verse? (*The Lord is speaking.*)

2) What are some of the things that God called Joseph Smith to do? (*Be a presiding elder, a translator, a revelator, and a prophet.*)

[Read the first part of D&C 135:3]

Joseph Smith, the Prophet and Seer of the Lord, has done more, save Jesus only, for the salvation of men in this world, than any other man that ever lived in it.

1) What is "salvation?" (*It means that we overcome sin and death through Jesus Christ.*)

2) What are some things that Joseph Smith did to bring salvation to others? (*He brought people to Jesus Christ by translating the Book of Mormon, restoring the church, restoring the priesthood to perform ordinances such as baptism, and he taught others about Jesus Christ.*)

3) How has Joseph Smith's works helped to bring you closer to Jesus Christ? (*Discuss.*)

[Read the first part of D&C 135:1]

To seal the testimony of this book and the Book of Mormon, we announce the martyrdom of Joseph Smith the Prophet, and Hyrum Smith the Patriarch. They were shot in Carthage jail, on the 27th of June, 1844, about five o'clock p.m.

1) How did Joseph Smith die? *(He was shot and killed by an angry mob while he was in Carthage Jail.)*

2) What is a "martyr?" *(Someone who is killed because of their beliefs.)*

ACTIVITY PAGES:

[Pass out the Coloring Page]

Invite the children to color the Joseph Smith coloring page or to complete the Joseph Smith dot-to-dot activity. Use this time to talk about how you have been blessed by the work that Joseph Smith did.

♡ TESTIMONY:

Bear testimony of the truths found in the scriptures.

This page intentionally left blank.

Joseph Smith was a prophet of God

Cut out the squares on the grey lines and shuffle them. Have children work together to assemble the puzzle!

This page intentionally left blank.

Joseph Smith was a prophet of God

This page intentionally left blank.

Joseph Smith was a prophet of God

This page intentionally left blank.

LATTER DAY
KIDS

Week 49: Dec 1-7

 D&C 137-138

 TOPIC | Baptism for the Dead

 OPENING SONG "Baptism"

 **PREPARATION:**

You will need some oven mitts, and some string.

💬 INTRODUCTION ACTIVITY:

Put on the oven mitts, and attempt to tie a knot in the string (this should be impossible). Now ask if there is anyone who can "be your helping hands" and help you tie a knot in the string! Allow each child to make a knot in the string for you.

Once the activity is complete, discuss the following questions:

1) Was I able to tie a knot in the string by myself? (*No.*)

2) Why not? (*The gloves prevented you from using your hands.*)

3) Is there a knot in the string now? (*Yes.*)

4) How did that happen? (*Other people were able to act as your hands and tie the knot for you!*)

Explain: God has said that everyone must be baptized for the remission of sins. But, some people have died without having a chance to be baptized! Those people don't have a body any more (they only have a spirit), and they can't be baptized right now even if they want to! Just like I couldn't tie these shoes!

But, God has provided a way for those spirits to still be baptized! Since we have a body, we can volunteer to be baptized for them! Just like you used your hands to tie a knot in this string for me!

▶️ VIDEO:

Say: "Now we are going to watch a story about a boy who has a grandpa who never got baptized. The boy learns about baptisms for the dead. Let's watch and see what the boy learns."

[Watch Video: "What About Grandpa? | A Story About Baptisms for the Dead"]

Discuss the following questions after watching the video:

1) Why couldn't the boy's grandpa be baptized for himself? (*Because he didn't have a body.*)

2) How did the boy's grandpa learn about Jesus Christ? (*Missionaries in the spirit world taught him about Jesus Christ.*)

3) If the grandpa doesn't have a body any more, how can he be baptized? (*Someone with a body can be baptized for him!*)

4) Where are the baptismal fonts that are used for people in the spirit world? (*Inside the temple.*)

📖 SCRIPTURE:

Read the following scriptures and discuss the questions that follow.

[Read D&C 138:30]

But behold, from among the righteous, he organized his forces and appointed messengers, clothed with power and authority, and commissioned them to go forth and carry the light of the gospel to them that were in darkness, even to all the spirits of men; and thus was the gospel preached to the dead.

1) Who preached the gospel to the dead? (*Messengers who had power and authority.*)

2) Who sent the messengers to teach the gospel? (*Jesus Christ.*)

[Read D&C 138:33]

These were taught faith in God, repentance from sin, vicarious baptism for the remission of sins, the gift of the Holy Ghost by the laying on of hands...

1) What are some of the things that the missionaries teach about in the spirit world?" (*Faith in God, repentance from sin, baptisms for the dead, and the gift of the Holy Ghost.*)

[Read 1 Peter 4:6]

For for this cause was the gospel preached also to them that are dead, that they might be judged according to men in the flesh, but live according to God in the spirit.

1) How can the people who are dead learn about the gospel? (*They are taught about the gospel in the spirit world.*)

2) Can they be baptized when they don't have a body? (*No.*)

3) How can they be baptized? (*Someone who is still living can be baptized for them!*)

ACTIVITY PAGES:

[Pass out the Coloring Page]

Invite the children to color the scene from the video. Use this time to talk about your ancestors, and vicarious baptisms for the dead.

♡ TESTIMONY:

Bear testimony of the truths found in the scriptures.

This page intentionally left blank.

This page intentionally left blank.

Week 50: Dec 8 - 14

 ARTICLES OF FAITH & OFFICIAL DECLARATION 1&2

 TOPIC | The Articles of Faith

OPENING SONG "I Will Follow God's Plan"

PREPARATION:

Each child will need some kind of small box to serve as a "treasure box." Print the "Treasure Up" activity page (once copy for each child). Before the lesson begins, print an extra copy of the "Treasure Up" activity page and cut out the thirteen diamonds. Hide the diamonds around the room.

💬 INTRODUCTION ACTIVITY:

When you begin the lesson, tell the children they will be going on a treasure hunt! Invite all of the children to search the room together until they find all thirteen diamonds! After they have found all of the diamonds, spread them out in a place where everyone can see them.

Explain: Knowing what is true is a great treasure! If we believe something that is true, then we have power to make good choices! But if we believe something that is not true, we can waste a lot of time doing the wrong things.

Today we are going to learn about thirteen treasures of truth that the prophet Joseph Smith taught us! These thirteen treasures of truth are called "The Articles of Faith!"

▶ VIDEO + ACTIVITY:

First, pass out one activity page to each child. Help each child cut out their thirteen diamonds and place them in a pile next to that child's treasure box.

Now, say: "We are going to go on another treasure hunt! We are going to watch a video about the thirteen Articles of Faith! Remember, each one of these is a treasure of truth! Every time you discover one of the treasures, you get to put a diamond in your treasure box!"

[Watch Video: "The Articles of Faith | Animated Scripture Lesson for Kids"]

Discuss the following questions after watching the video:

1) Why is it important to know what is true? *(Because if we believe something that is true, we have power to make good choices.)*

2) What happens if we believe in something that is not true? *(We can waste a lot of time doing the wrong things.)*

3) What treasures of truth did you find when you were watching the video? *(Discuss a few of the Articles of Faith that the children remember.)*

4) Who wrote the Articles of Faith? *(Joseph Smith wrote them in a letter to tell someone what we believe.)*

SCRIPTURE:

Read the following scriptures and discuss the questions that follow.

[Read the last part of Alma 17:2]

...and they had waxed strong in the knowledge of the truth; for they were men of a sound understanding and they had searched the scriptures diligently, that they might know the word of God.

1) Who are these scripture talking about? *(The sons of Mosiah, while they were doing missionary work.)*

2) What does it mean to "wax strong" in the knowledge of truth? *(It means they understood the truth really well and they were able to make lots of good choices.)*

3) How did they learn so much about truth? *(They searched the scriptures diligently.)*

[Read John 8:32-34]

And ye shall know the truth, and the truth shall make you free.

1) What can make us free? (*Knowing the truth will make us free!*)

♡ TESTIMONY:

Bear testimony of the truths found in the scriptures.

This page intentionally left blank.

"Treasure up in your minds continually the words of life..."

-D&C 84:85

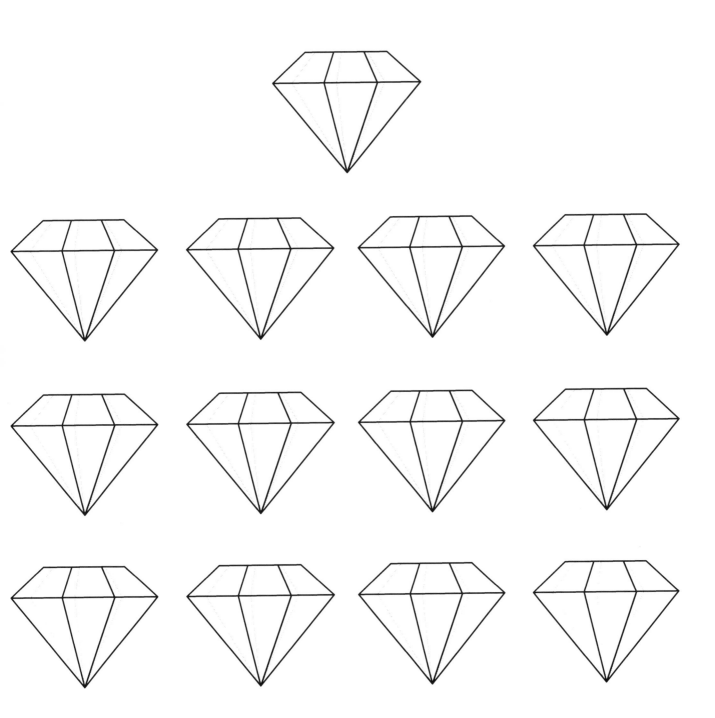

Cut out each of the diamons and place them in a pile. Watch the video "The Articles of Faith | Animated Scripture Lesson for Kids." Follow along with the video and each time you "discover" another treasure of truth, place another diamond in your treasure box! (As an alternative, you could choose to color in one of the diamonds each time you discover another treasure of truth!)

This page intentionally left blank.

Week 51: Dec 15 - 21

 THE FAMILY: A PROCLAMATION TO THE WORLD

 TOPIC | The Family Proclamation

OPENING SONG "Families Can Be Together Forever"

 **PREPARATION:**

You will need several popsicle sticks and two rubber bands.

INTRODUCTION ACTIVITY:

Scatter the popsicle sticks around the room. Hold up one of the popsicle sticks and ask for a volunteer to try to break the stick. After the stick is broken, explain that we are like the popsicle sticks, and we are in a battle! Heavenly Father wants to give us life and salvation, but the enemy of righteousness wants to "break" us and destroy our happiness!

Now ask the following questions:

1) What do you think will happen to all of these popsicle sticks if the enemy tries to break them one at a time? *(They will break easily.)*

2) Do you think Heavenly Father wants us to be alone in this battle like these popsicle sticks? *(No! He wants us to be in families!)*

3) What do you think will happen if we gather the popsicle sticks together in a strong family? *(The enemy won't be able to break them!)*

Now invite the children to gather all of the popsicle sticks together and to use the rubber bands to "bind" them together into a family unit. Let the children take turns trying to break the "family!"

▶ VIDEO:

Now we are going to watch a video about families! Heavenly Father wants us to live in families, and he has taught us many things we can do to build a strong family! Let's see how many things you can remember!

[Watch Video: "The Family Proclamation | Animated Scripture Lesson for Kids"]

Discuss the following questions after watching the video:

1) What are some of the things you remember that can make our families stronger? *(Discuss.)*

2) Is it easy or hard to build a strong family? *(It can be hard, and it can take a long time!)*

3) If it's hard to build a strong family, does that mean we should stop trying to build a strong family? *(No! We should keep trying to build a strong family!)*

4) Why do you think Heavenly Father wants us to live in families? *(Discuss.)*

📖 SCRIPTURE:

Read the following scriptures and discuss the questions that follow.

[3 Nephi 18:21]

Pray in your families unto the Father, always in my name, that your wives and your children may be blessed.

1) Who is speaking in this verse? *(Jesus Christ is speaking.)*

2) Why do you think Jesus Christ told us to pray in our families? *(Discuss.)*

[Read the first part of 1 Nephi 1:1]

I, Nephi, having been born of goodly parents, therefore I was taught somewhat in all the learning of my father...

1) Who taught Nephi the things that he needed to know? *(His parents.)*

2) Do you think that Nephi was stronger because of his family? *(Discuss.)*

[Read Alma 56:47-48]

Now they never had fought, yet they did not fear death; and they did think more upon the liberty of their fathers than they did upon their lives; yea, they had been taught by their mothers, that if they did not doubt, God would deliver them. And they rehearsed unto me the words of their mothers, saying: We do not doubt our mothers knew it.

    1) Who taught the stripling warriors? *(Their mothers!)*

    2) What did their mothers teach them to do? *(To have faith in God and not doubt.)*

 ## ACTIVITY PAGES:

[Pass out coloring page]

Invite children to complete the "Families" activity page. Use this time to talk about families, and why families are important to Heavenly Father.

♡ TESTIMONY:

Bear testimony of the truths found in the scriptures.

This page intentionally left blank.

We are all spirit sons and daughters of Heavenly Parents. Families are central to the Creator's Plan!

Draw the members of your family in the space below, together with your heavenly parents!

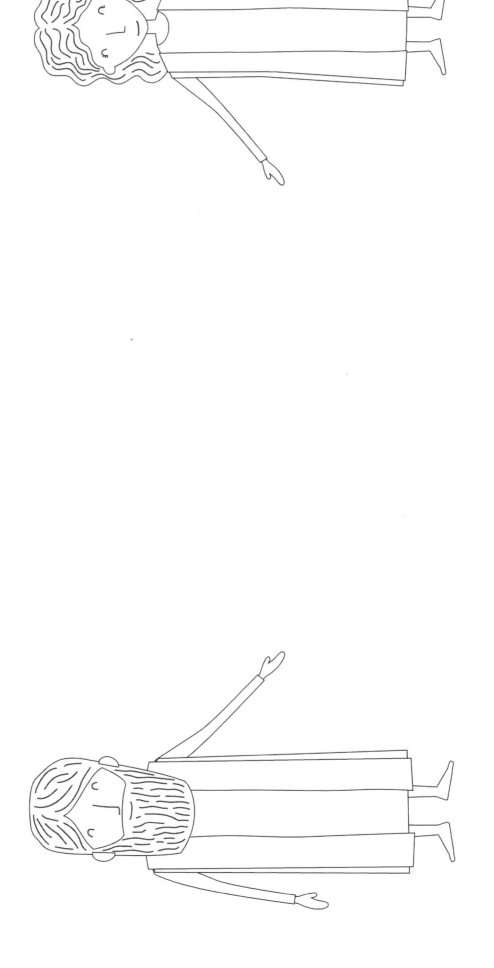

This page intentionally left blank.

Week 52: Dec 22 - 28

 **CHRISTMAS**

 **TOPIC** | The Symbols of Christmas

OPENING SONG | "Away in a Manger"

PREPARATION:

You will need several sheets of paper and some scissors. Cut a large heart shape out of one of the papers. Cut several other large shapes out of the remaining sheets of paper (rectangle, triangle, circle, square, star, etc.).

INTRODUCTION ACTIVITY:

Place all of the shapes in a row in front of the children so that everyone can see them. Then discuss the following questions:

1) If you wanted to say "I love you" to someone without using words, what shape would you want to give to them? *(The heart shape!)*

2) Why would you choose the heart shape? *(Discuss.)*

Explain: The heart shape is a symbol for love! Symbols can help us understand many things and they can help us remember things too! When Heavenly Father teaches us, He often uses symbols! Today we are going to learn about some of the symbols of Christmas!

VIDEO:

Now we are going to watch a video about the symbols of Christmas! See if you can remember what the symbols mean!

343

[Watch Video: "The Symbols of Christmas | Animated Scripture Lesson for Kids"]

Discuss the following questions after watching the video:

1) What symbols do you remember? (*Discuss.*)

2) What do all of the Christmas symbols make us think about? (*Jesus Christ!*)

3) Can you think of other symbols that help us remember Jesus Christ? (*The cross, the bread and water when we take the sacrament, etc.*)

4) Why do you think Heavenly Father wants us to remember Jesus Christ? (*Because we need Him!*)

 # SCRIPTURE:

Read the following scriptures and discuss the questions that follow.

[John 8:12]

Then spake Jesus again unto them, saying, I am the light of the world: he that followeth me shall not walk in darkness, but shall have the light of life.

1) Who is the light of the world? (*Jesus Christ!*)

2) What does it mean to walk in darkness? (*It means that we don't know what to do or where to go. We are lost.*)

3) What does it mean to have the light of Christ in our life? (*It means we will see the truth and we will know where to do and what to do!*)

4) What Christmas symbol reminds us that Jesus Christ is the light of the world? (*Christmas lights!*)

[3 Nephi 1:20-21]

And it had come to pass, yea, all things, every whit, according to the words of the prophets. And it came to pass also that a new star did appear, according to the word.

1) What did the prophets say would happen when Christ was born? (*They said a new star would appear!*)

1) What happened when Christ was born? (*A new star appeared!*)

2) Who saw the new star? (*Everyone was able to see it!*)

3) What Christmas symbol reminds us about the new star? (*The star on the top of the tree.*)

[Watch the video: "The Nativity Story | Animated Scripture Lesson for Kids"]

[Read John 3:16]

For God so loved the world, that he gave his only begotten Son, that whosoever believeth in him should not perish, but have everlasting life.

1) What gift did God give to the world? (*He gave His only begotten Son, Jesus Christ.*)

2) Why did God give us the gift of Jesus Christ? (*Because He loved us so much.*)

3) What Christmas symbol reminds us of the gift that God gave us? (*Christmas presents!*)

ACTIVITY PAGES:

[Pass out coloring page]

Invite children to complete the "Christmas Symbols" matching activity. Use this time to talk about Jesus Christ, and why His birth and His atonement are so important to us.

TESTIMONY:

Bear testimony of the truths found in the scriptures.

This page intentionally left blank.

Symbols of Christmas

Color the ornaments, then cut them out. Match them with their meanings by gluing them to the matching symbols on the second page.

This page intentionally left blank.

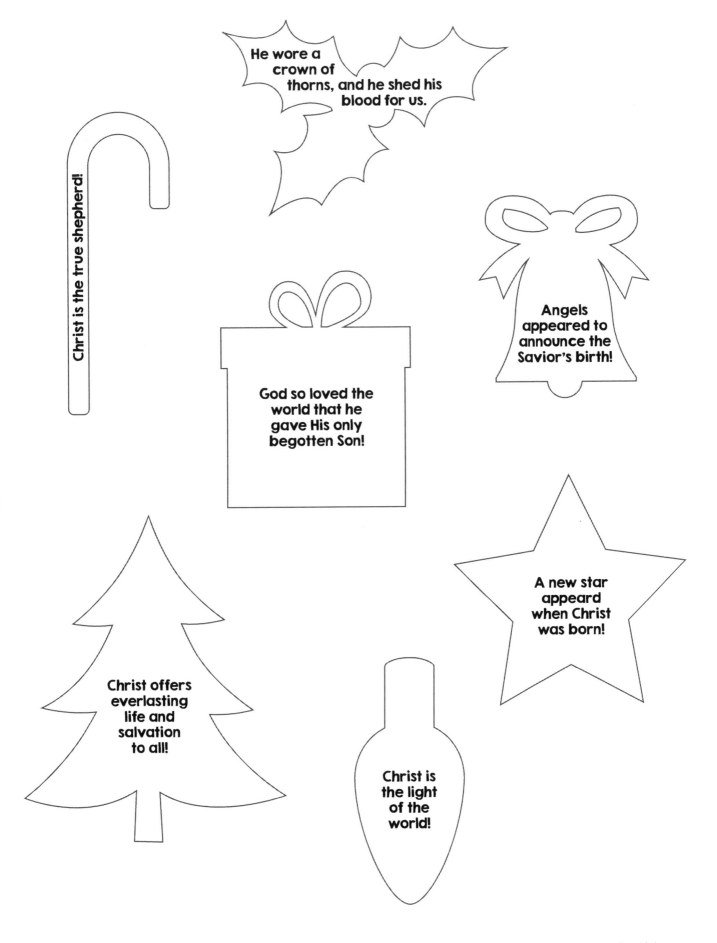

He wore a crown of thorns, and he shed his blood for us.

Christ is the true shepherd!

Angels appeared to announce the Savior's birth!

God so loved the world that he gave His only begotten Son!

A new star appeard when Christ was born!

Christ offers everlasting life and salvation to all!

Christ is the light of the world!

This page intentionally left blank.

Made in United States
Troutdale, OR
12/15/2024

26596280R00201